Teaching Adults

Amanda Hayes

continuum

Continuum International Publishing Group
The Tower Building   80 Maiden Lane
11 York Road   Suite 704
London   New York
SE1 7NX   NY 10038

British Library Cataloguing-in-Publication Data
A catalogue record for this book is available from the British Library.

ISBN: 0–8264–8707–6 (paperback)

Typeset by YHT Ltd
Printed and bound in Great Britain by, Ashford Colour Press Ltd, Gosport, Hampshire.

Contents

Series foreword

THE ESSENTIAL FE TOOLKIT SERIES

Jill Jameson
Series Editor

In the autumn of 1974, a young woman newly arrived from Africa landed in Devon to embark on a new life in England. Having travelled half way round the world, she still longed for sunny Zimbabwe. Not sure what career to follow, she took a part-time job teaching EFL to Finnish students. Having enjoyed this, she studied thereafter for a PGCE at the University of Nottingham in Ted Wragg's Education Department. After teaching in secondary schools, she returned to university in Cambridge, and, after graduating, took a job in ILEA in 1984 in adult education. She loved it: there was something about adult education that woke her up, made her feel fully alive, newly aware of all the lifelong learning journeys being followed by so many students and staff around her. The adult community centre she worked in was a joyful place for diverse multi-ethnic communities. Everyone was cared for, including 90-year-olds in wheelchairs, toddlers in the crèche, ESOL refugees, city accountants in business suits and university level graphic design students. In her eyes, the centre was an educational ideal, a remarkable place in which, gradually, everyone was helped to learn to be who they wanted to be. This was the Chequer Centre, Finsbury, EC1, the 'red house', as her daughter saw it, toddling in from the crèche. And so began the story of a long interest in further education that was to last for many years . . . why, if they did such good work for so many, were FE centres so under-funded and unrecognized, so under-appreciated?

It is with delight that, 32 years after the above story began, I write the Foreword to *The Essential FE Toolkit*, Continuum's new series of 24 books on further education (FE) for teachers and college leaders. The idea behind the *Toolkit* is to provide a comprehensive guide to FE in a series of compact, readable books. The suite of 24 individual books are gathered together to provide the practitioner with an overall FE toolkit in specialist, fact-filled volumes designed to be easily accessible, written by experts with significant knowledge and experience in their individual fields. All of the authors have in-depth understanding of further education. But 'Why is further education important? Why does it merit a whole series to be written about it?' you may ask.

At the Association of Colleges Annual Conference in 2005, in a humorous speech to college principals, John Brennan said that, whereas in 1995 further education was a 'political backwater', by 2005 it had become 'mainstream'. John recalled that since 1995 there had been '36 separate Government or Government-sponsored reports or white papers specifically devoted to the post-16 sector'. In our recent regional research report (2006) for the Learning and Skills Development Agency, my co-author Yvonne Hillier and I noted that it was no longer 'raining policy' in FE, as we had described earlier (Jameson and Hillier, 2003): there is now a torrent of new initiatives. We thought in 2003 that an umbrella would suffice to protect you. We'd now recommend buying a boat to navigate these choppy waters, as it looks as if John Brennan's 'mainstream' FE, combined with a tidal wave of government policies will soon lead to a flood of new interest in the sector, rather than end anytime soon.

There are good reasons for all this government attention on further education. In 2004/2005, student numbers in LSC-funded further education increased to 4.2m, total college income was around £6.1 billion, and the average college had an annual turnover of £15m. Further education has rapidly increased in national significance regarding the need for ever greater achievements in UK education and skills training for millions of learners, providing qualifications and workforce training to feed a UK national economy hungrily in competition with other OECD nations. The 120 recommendations of the Foster Review (2005) therefore in the main encourage colleges to focus their work on vocational skills, social inclusion and achieving academic progress. This series is here to consider all three of these areas and more.

The series is written for teaching practitioners, leaders and managers in the 572 FE/LSC-funded institutions in the UK, including FE colleges, adult education and sixth form institutions, prison education departments, training and workforce development units, local education authorities and community agencies. The series is also written for PGCE/Cert Ed/City & Guilds Initial and continuing professional development (CPD) teacher trainees in universities in the UK, USA, Canada, Australia, New Zealand and beyond. It will also be of interest to staff in the 600 Jobcentre Plus providers in the UK and to many private training organisations. All may find this series of use and interest in learning about FE educational practice in the 24 different areas of these specialist books from experts in the field.

Our use of this somewhat fuzzy term 'practitioners' includes staff in the FE/LSC-funded sector who engage in professional practice in governance, leadership, management, teaching, training, financial and administration services, student support services, ICT and MIS technical support, librarianship, learning resources, marketing, research and development, nursery and crèche services, community and business support, transport and estates management. It is also intended to include staff in a host of other FE services including work-related training, catering, outreach and specialist health, diagnostic additional learning support, pastoral and religious support for students. Updating staff in professional practice is critically important at a time of such continuing radical policy-driven change, and we are pleased to contribute to this nationally and internationally.

We are also privileged to have an exceptional range of authors writing for the series. Many of our series authors are renowned for their work in further education, having worked in the sector for thirty years or more. Some have received OBE or CBE honours, professorships, fellowships and awards for contributions they have made to further education. All have demonstrated a commitment to FE that makes their books come alive with a kind of wise guidance for the reader. Sometimes this is tinged with world-weariness, sometimes with sympathy, humour or excitement. Sometimes the books are just plain clever or a fascinating read, to guide practitioners of the future who will read these works. Together, the books make up a considerable portfolio of assets for you to take with you through your journeys in further education. We hope the experience of reading the books will be interesting, instructive and pleasurable and that experience gained from them will last, renewed, for many seasons.

It has been wonderful to work with all of the authors and with Continuum's UK Education Publisher, Alexandra Webster, on this series. The exhilarating opportunity of developing such a comprehensive toolkit of books probably comes once in a lifetime, if at all. I am privileged to have had this rare opportunity, and I thank the publishers, authors and other contributors to the series for making these books come to life with their fantastic contributions to FE.

Dr Jill Jameson
Series Editor
March, 2006

Series introduction

Teaching Adults – Amanda Hayes

This book on Teaching Adults provides a wide-ranging guide to inform readers about why adults have different needs from younger students, including the requirement for a flexibly tailored curriculum. Amanda Hayes, the author, is a Fellow of the Royal Society of Arts, a PhD graduate in Education from King's College, London, and Vice-Principal of Kensington and Chelsea College, which has more than 26,000 students (16,300 FE and 9,347 ACL).

Amanda guides us confidently and sensitively through the maze of complex issues we need to consider in providing an effective teaching environment for adult learners. She examines the political, social and economic drivers for increasing the number of adults in FE and reports on current government priorities for the education and training of adults. She considers the need for flexible teaching methods, including distance learning, and the relative merits of mixed age or discrete provision. Amanda advises us on recruitment and selection strategies, providing guidelines for learning and teaching which really help adult students to succeed. Motivators to inspire adult students and give them confidence are considered in depth, as is the role of mentoring and peer mentoring. Methods for efficient early identification of academic and pastoral support needs are described. Advice on different learning styles and equality and diversity in recruitment, the curriculum and in learning materials is provided.

Amanda feels it is important to have an holistic approach to the teaching of adults, and to know the limits of your responsibilities as a teacher. She examines and reports on work skills teaching for adults, including workplace learning and assessment, and the use of learning pathways and personal development. She recommends 'best practice' in teaching adults overall and describes methods of teaching in a range of venues, including community education venues. Amanda gives us a useful overview of issues that can be a problem for adult learners, including family and financial responsibilities, so that students can best be supported to achieve and progress. Amanda provides us with a range of follow-up and in-depth resources for teaching adults. This is an outstandingly useful book for lecturers, teachers, tutors and trainers of adult learners, and will prove to be essential reading for a long time to come.

Dr Jill Jameson
Director of Research
School of Education and Training
University of Greenwich
j.jameson@gre.ac.uk

Acknowledgements

I should like to thank the many colleagues and students who have shared their learning journeys with me, and whose experiences of what makes a positive adult learning experience are at the heart of this book.

I am grateful to Jill Jameson for her wise counsel and Alexandra Webster for her boundless enthusiasm for this book and the series as a whole.

'Did I miss anything?' reprinted by permission of the author and Harbour Publishing Co Ltd.

Finally, I owe a huge debt of gratitude to my own 'adult learners' Tony, Emily, James and Nick for their honest feedback and support throughout the research and writing stages of this project.

Introduction

Teaching adults is a privilege and a delight. Nothing can beat the feeling of seeing students, many of whom have not flourished in their previous educational experiences, gain new skills and confidence and embark on a positive new phase of their lives. Teaching adults is challenging not only because of the broad range of life experiences students bring into the class, but because of the professional expectations that government and its agencies have of us.

Although education and training for adults have a long tradition, adults did not have a statutory right to publicly funded education until the 1992 Further and Higher Education Act. In the years that have followed, further education (FE) has been a site of radical transformation, the changes being driven by government policy initiatives in response to social and economic factors. The expansion in the number of adults accessing post-compulsory education, especially award-bearing courses, has been considerable. There are now approximately 1.7 million students enrolled on learning programmes in the sector as a whole. They are studying with FE colleges, Local Education Authorities (LEAs), the voluntary sector and private trainers, who between them offer a rich range of subjects and modes of study across levels from beginner to post-qualification.

Government policy has focused on three key priorities: first, developing industrial training to increase Britain's skill base in order to develop the nation's economic competitive strength; second, widening participation in education by people who have few or no formal qualifications, in order to get them into employment and not dependent on welfare payments; and third, finding strategies that encourage social inclusion and reduce crime. Education providers have been under pressure from government to respond to these priorities and at the same time to achieve high academic standards and raise levels of student retention and achievement. We need continuously to reflect on our practice and find ways to be more effective.

Adult learning takes place in a range of contexts, including: formal accredited vocational and academic provision in colleges; non-qualification-bearing courses in colleges and community venues; work-based learning; and informal learning through clubs and societies, television and the Internet. It may also be experienced in a variety of full and part-time modes.

In the chapters that follow, we will consider what it means to be an adult student and identify strategies that we can use, as lecturers and managers of adult learning, to make our provision – in whatever context – relevant and enjoyable.

The sector benefits from the skills and enthusiasm of numerous staff who are practising professionals in their own field and may not yet be qualified teachers. Changing curriculum priorities also mean that we all need to be confident and competent to work with different groups from those we may have taught in the past. I have therefore not made any assumptions about the amount of experience the reader has had of teaching, or working with, adults. The emphasis is on understanding the expectations and needs of our students so that we can help them succeed. We will therefore take a cultural approach[1] to learning that links practice to the wider social context. Although teaching and learning strategies will be discussed, it is not my intention to be prescriptive, or to be heavily focused on teaching theory or techniques. While there are commonalities between organisations delivering FE, the cultures of each learning site are different from each other, indeed they may differ from one department to another, so the best practice advice is offered as a possible approach rather than a 'must do'.

It is beyond the scope of this book to take a detailed theoretical approach to adult learning, but some recent relevant research and data sources are detailed in the text and end notes

---

[1] For further reading on learning cultures see Wertsch 1998; Bourdieu 1977 and 1982; Lave and Wenger 1991.

to enable those of you who are undertaking research, perhaps as part of a teacher training qualification, to follow up issues in more depth.

We are all adult learners, as well as educators. If we keep this thought central to our practice, learn from colleagues and our students and share our knowledge, then success and enjoyment are assured.

1 Why adult students are different

What do we mean by an adult learner?

Adulthood has been differently defined over time and across cultures. In the context of this book, I am using the term 'adult student' to be the Learning and Skills Council (LSC) definition of someone over nineteen years of age. School education caters for the ages 5 to 18, a span of 13 years. Within each school class, all pupils are approximately the same age. The age span in adult classes in FE and Adult Community Learning (ACL) tends to be very different. I have, for example, taught adult classes in which the student ages have spanned some 60 years. This is one of the reasons that our sector is so very interesting to work in, but the difference in students' age and maturity needs to be taken into account when planning and delivering the curriculum if it is to be a positive experience for everyone.

We often hear the phrases 'adult learner' and 'non-learners'. People continue to learn throughout their lives, often through informal experiences, and therefore in my view there is no such category as 'non-learners'. There are, however, people who choose not to engage in formal education and training. Their non-engagement may be due to a variety of factors, including a feeling that education has no relevance to their lives or that they are no good at it. Referring to this group as 'non-learners' simply reinforces this self-image. The project of successive governments has been to promote a culture of lifelong learning[1] in which adults can continue to develop new skills and thereby social justice and a strong national economy can be achieved. Thus people with few qualifications and low basic skills have been prioritized. It is important that organizations in the learning and skills sector find ways to encourage these people to return to education and to see themselves as 'adult learners'.

Why adults return to education

What motivates someone to return to education in adulthood? There are obviously a variety of social, economic and educational reasons. For women, college can be a break from childcare, enabling them to have social contact with adults and find a space to re-assert their individuality. New skills and qualifications also open up the possibility of a better job and improved lifestyle. Some students have a clear aim, perhaps gaining a new or higher level qualification, such as hairdressing NVQ level 3, or the European Computer Driving Licence. I describe these kinds of learners as 'specific focus students'. Others articulate the desire to return to learning as 'wanting to feel better about myself', 'wanting my life to be more rewarding'. Their return is often linked to a change of personal circumstances, such as children leaving home, divorce, bereavement or redundancy. These 'life changers' are looking for something more from themselves and from the course than a straight qualification. There are also students who receive training organized by their employers and provided by FE colleges either in the workplace or on release to college.

The prior experience of adult students can vary considerably, especially on a non-accredited course where you may have highly educated and qualified people learning alongside people with no qualifications. This mix of level, ability, individual motivation and self-confidence in their ability to learn is what makes working with adults so interesting. However, for it to be a good experience for everyone, it will need managing by you as the teacher or curriculum manager.

All students need good quality initial guidance to help them choose the most appropriate programme of study and ongoing support. We shall discuss this in more depth in Chapter 7. However, it must not be forgotten that what students want from education alters as a result of the learning process and the changing demands and priorities in their lives. Ongoing review of achievement and aims is therefore important.

Can you teach an old dog new tricks?

There are numerous myths and misconceptions about the impact of ageing on the capacity to learn. In later years, memory (such as the ability to recall names quickly) can diminish or be erratic, but a fit and healthy person continues to learn new things effectively in adulthood (Withnall *et al.*, 2004). As they learn, people pass through a number of cognitive developmental stages. With adults, as with children, it is often more useful to think of 'stages' rather than ages (see *Teaching the FE Curriculum* by Mark Weyers in this series).

Preferred learning styles

In recent years, there has been a shift in emphasis in inspection from reviewing systems to looking at the impact policies and procedures have on the individual student. There is more focus on learning than teaching, and rightly so: there is no point in being an 'expert' in something if we cannot make it interesting and relevant to our students.

Teacher trainers and the inspectorate have encouraged the use of 'learning styles' instruments, which are now widely used in higher and further education by lecturers keen to match teaching and learning activities to the preferences of individual students. The Learning and Skills Research Centre (LSRC) has shown that a reliable and valid instrument that measures learning styles could be used as a tool to diagnose how people learn and show them how to enhance their learning. Work with learning styles can also provide learners with a much needed 'lexicon of learning' – a language with which to discuss their own learning preferences and those of others. It can reveal how people learn or fail to learn, and how lecturers can facilitate or hinder these processes. However, this research has also drawn attention to the proliferation of concepts, instruments and pedagogical strategies that suggests 'conceptual confusion, the serious failure of accumulated theoretical coherence and the absence of well-grounded findings, tested through replication' (Coffield *et al.* 2004). This research states that current 'self report' instruments are not robust enough because they are sampling not the behaviour of learners but only their impressions of how they learn: impressions which may be inaccurate, self-deluding or influenced by what the respondent thinks the tester wants to hear. So while students certainly respond better to some learning situations than to others, great caution should be applied in seeing current learning styles instruments as 'scientific' and 'the answer' in all contexts. Experience suggests that for students of any age, the most effective strategies are to reinforce learning through a wide range of stimuli and activities and to ensure that we check individual understanding and competence, giving regular feedback and offering support and encouragement.

Education in the 'school of life'

Compared with children, adults have a vast wealth of knowledge, gained in formal and informal settings, which they bring to new learning situations. They have considerable experience of the process of acquiring knowledge and skills and putting it to practical use, usually as the result of day-to-day problem solving.

Unlike students in a school classroom, students on an FE course may be from different generations. They may also have received their initial education in a different country. As a result, their cultures and previous experiences of education may affect their attitudes to teaching and learning and the types of relationships they feel it is appropriate to have with staff and other students. For many students, being invited to share their life experiences in the class is a positive experience that enables them to feel they have something valuable to contribute and share with the group. For others, it is a threat, an invasion of privacy and a situation in which their worst fears of exposing their inadequacies may come to the fore. Badly handled, an invitation to students to contribute in class can re-kindle memories of former public humiliation and failure. Describing her reason for dropping out of a previous course, one woman wrote, 'The teacher was awful and made me feel inadequate and foolish.' We need to get to know our students and build up trust within the group before we 'put them on the spot', however well-intentioned our actions are. We must also be sensitive: we do not know the personal circumstances of individuals. Topics such as abusive relationships, politics and religion will always need to be carefully handled.

Let us now think about the most important things to bear in mind when teaching adults. A key test I use when observing classes is to ask myself if a family member, such as my mother, would enjoy it, or if I would like to be there myself. I then analyse the reasons for this response, starting with the question, 'Does the lecturer value their students' adult experience and accumulated knowledge?' This is essential, as it helps engage adults and makes them feel respected and motivated. Although we have expertise in our field, some students may also have skills and knowledge in this area that can be drawn out. We need to help them make connections between what they already know and what they are currently learning in our class. They are not empty vessels to have information from us 'poured in' (Lave and Wenger 1991).[2] However, we need to develop interesting ways to draw out theory from practice. Adults who have not been engaged in any formal education or training for a number of years will have absorbed knowledge and gained skills through experience. Their learning may, therefore, not be underpinned by any formal theories. This does not mean that they have not identified some principles through trial and error, which they have been able to apply in different circumstances. They may know that something works: our role is to help them understand why.

We should never make assumptions about adult students, either about what they know or about what they do not know. Life has taught them to protect themselves physically and emotionally. They do not want to fail or to look foolish in front of other people. We need to be sensitive to situations in which a student may be struggling but is reluctant to ask for help. Asking the group, 'OK, so did you all understand that?', and then moving on, is not the same thing as checking that learning is taking place. Students with gaps in their literacy, numeracy and language abilities have often learnt how to hide these deficiencies.

After a day at work, adult students sometimes see an evening class as a time to relax, but whatever time of day we teach, we need to ensure that students move on in their learning. We need to challenge them to try something new, such as a technique, or to consider a new idea or alternative set of values, but we need to do this sensitively. Suggesting that our students need to modify their attitudes can be a danger area. However, it may be important to do this if what they believe is 'a well-known fact' is now an old idea that has been scientifically disproved, or is part of a discriminatory discourse such as sexism or racism.

We need to encourage our students to be autonomous learners through our teaching style and methods. Any class of adults is likely to encompass students with a wide range of skills, with confident and competent learners who are updating, or moving into a new vocational area, alongside those who are slower at absorbing new things, or who have been out of education for a long time and therefore are not confident or independent learners.

Getting the balance right between giving people information and helping them to acquire it themselves through research and interaction with others is crucial, and can be difficult. Adults have different expectations depending on their previous experiences of education. There are some adults whose initial schooling has led them to expect you to tell them what to do and to be very directive. I have known student evaluations of the same class to include comments that the lecturer should have been both more and less directive. So we need to exercise judgement. Similarly, adults have different reactions to our management or facilitation of their learning. They may say that they expect us to suggest ways of working and correct poor techniques, but maturity and independence in their everyday lives means that adults will sometimes not respond well to being told what to do and how to do it!

To get the best out of our students, we need to see the whole person. As we shall see in Chapter 7, there are many competing demands in adults' lives. Attending college and completing assignments at home has to be fitted around the pressures of family and work. This does not mean that lateness, intermittent attendance or non-completion of coursework is acceptable. It does, however, mean that students may need help managing the different demands on them.

Finally, we need to remember to recognize the wider personal and social benefits of learning in adulthood, which include meeting new people, increased cultural understanding and tolerance, and improved health (Feinstein *et al.*, 2003). When asked how returning to learning has impacted on their lives, adult students often talk about their gains in confidence and increased self-esteem. These personal outcomes are as significant as new subject skills and knowledge, but are rather more difficult to measure. However, recognising achievement of such intangible learning goals is not impossible, as will be discussed in Chapter 8.

Checklist for successful adult learning

- Value adults' experience and their accumulated knowledge.
- Help them make connections between what they already know and what they are currently learning in your class.
- Challenge them to try something new, but do it sensitively.
- Encourage them to be autonomous learners through your style and methods.
- Develop an environment of equal status: adults may not respond well to being told by you what to do and how to do it.
- Develop interesting ways to draw out theory from practice.
- Never make assumptions about adult students' skills or understanding: always check that learning is taking place.
- Remember to plan for and recognize the wider personal and social benefits of learning.
- See the whole person and support them to manage the different demands in their lives.

Adult students' expectations of the course

As we are all aware, adult students are generally busy people with commitments in a variety of spheres: home, work and community. They have made an effort to enrol and attend our course and may well have paid a fee. They expect this effort to be recognized and they also expect to get value for money. Let us look at what this means and what we have to do to meet their expectations.[3]

Students, not unsurprisingly, expect their lecturers to have secure subject knowledge and to keep themselves up to date in their field of specialism and in professional teaching and learning skills. However, we all know of colleagues who have not been involved in regular vocational updating, or are not confident in the use of information learning technology (ILT) and e-learning. We also know of colleagues who are not 'up to speed' with embedding literacy, language and numeracy in their specialist area. National initiatives in Skills for Life and Continuing Professional Development underline the government's expectations of teachers' professional competence.[4]

Students expect to be taught by someone they can respect, who is passionate about their subject and inspires them. This is an area in which lecturers in FE and in ACL really excel because so many staff also work as professionals in the subjects they teach, such as photography, catering or journalism. Whatever subject we teach, we need to be exemplars of best and current practice. Who wants to be taught hairdressing by someone whose own hair is in poor condition, or art by someone who does not regularly visit galleries? One of the best things about teaching adult students is that they are genuinely interested in the subjects we teach and respond enthusiastically to discussion of relevant television programmes, the demonstration of a new technique, or a visit to a museum, theatre or business. So motivation is reciprocal.

We all need to guard against slipping into lax habits. Adults are not as forgiving as younger learners and they rightly expect their lecturers to exemplify the qualities we expect of them. This includes being prepared and punctual. Arriving late, wandering off in the middle of the class in order to do some photocopying or taking mobile telephone calls is not impressive; it also gives adult students 'permission' to behave in a sloppy way, or may give them the impression that we do not care. Adults expect to achieve their learning goals. We should never assume that these are identical to the course objectives. They may want to re-prioritize our course objectives. They may have additional objectives of their own. They are also likely, however good the pre-course information and induction, to discover new personal learning goals as a result of engaging with the subject matter. This is how it should be – enjoyable and effective learning opens up new ideas and possibilities. There will also be 'unexpected learning', which often occurs as a result of interaction with other adults: for example, useful information about the local area. Perhaps the most important learning of all is the respect for cultural diversity that arises naturally from many adult education classes and that benefits us all.

When the course is specifically vocational, such as a business studies qualification course, students are likely to expect some links with employers, such as work experience or industry visits. Adult students may even expect to get a good job at the end of the course (Walhberg and Gleeson 2003).

We need to ensure that students feel stimulated and involved. A good lecturer employs a variety of teaching methods and resources to ensure that all students are actively engaged throughout the session. Learning should be fun for them and for us. Engaging students results in the 'buzz' that makes everyone look forward to the next session. Even in classes such as art and design or IT, in which students may be working on their own assignments, we need to find opportunities for large and small group teaching – otherwise they might as well learn from a book or computer package at home.

Some courses for adults do not lead to a qualification, but because students attend for the love of learning and for their own development, this does not mean that they do not want regular feedback on what they have achieved and how they could make further progress. All students want and need feedback. Failure to meet this expectation can result in students losing commitment and leaving the course.

Although you may be teaching adults in a building used by younger students and there may even be some younger students in your class, the adults will expect to be taught in an environment that is conducive to learning and that reflects their status. This means having a clean, comfortable, warm, tidy and quiet learning environment. This is not necessarily easily achieved in an FE college with a substantial 16 to 18-year-old student intake. It is up to us to create the best learning environment we can with the resources available. The first rule of adult education is to move the furniture! If you have a non-workshop course, then the best layout is a circle or horseshoe. This is because everyone can see each other, which is good for discussion and lends an atmosphere of equality. Adult students also expect to have recreational facilities, especially a refreshment area not dominated by loud teenagers and their litter. There is a long tradition of lecturers taking their coffee and tea breaks with their adult students. This reinforces the ethos of equality of adult status. As many adult students attend on a part-time basis, I have always found it a useful informal opportunity to get to know them better. This may run counter to normal practice in your workplace, however, and it has to be a personal choice.

Finally, adult students, in common with the rest of us, expect to be treated with respect by all members of the college community. This means we need to manage the classroom so that some students do not dominate our time to the detriment of others. Offensive behaviour, whether intentional or not, must be dealt with swiftly and effectively. As teachers, we need to be sensitive and to make sure that our own behaviour does not slip – engaging in sarcasm, public humiliation, or being patronizing are sins that students will not forgive.

Some student expectations may not be reasonable. This may be because of inadequate information and advice before enrolment, leading to a mismatch between course aim and delivery and the student's prior experience and learning needs. If you can pick up a 'mismatch situation' quickly and transfer the student to a more appropriate course, this will prevent disappointment and possible drop-out. Unfortunately, some students have an unrealistic view of their own capabilities and are reluctant to modify their expectations and set themselves attainable goals. This will require good tutorial support and guidance to achieve a positive outcome. Do not be afraid to ask for the advice and support of colleagues in these situations.

Understanding our students' expectations helps to keep them individually motivated. If you build a cohesive group, you will find that adult students will support and encourage each other in a way you seldom get with younger people. Meeting the different expectations of a group of individuals is a challenge. It can take all our skill, experience and ingenuity. For example, students don't expect us to allow other students to disrupt their learning, yet they may be offended if we mention that their own lateness has just that effect on others. In the chapters that follow we will look at some ideas and techniques to help us not only to survive but also to thrive!

Checklist of adult students' expectations

Use this to plan and review your course

- To have lecturers with secure subject knowledge who are up to date in their field of specialism and their teaching skills.
- To be taught by someone who loves their subject and inspires them.
- To have competent lecturers who arrive punctually and properly prepared.
- To be stimulated and involved in a variety of learning activities which are fun.
- To achieve their personal learning goals – which may modify during the course.
- To have direct contact with employers/work experience on vocational courses.
- To have sufficient individual attention, but be part of a group learning exchange.
- To have regular feedback on what they have achieved and how they could make further progress.
- To be treated with respect by all members of the class

and have any offensive or disruptive behaviour managed quickly and effectively.

- To be taught in a clean, safe, comfortable, warm, tidy and quiet environment.
- To have recreational facilities, especially a refreshment area that is not dominated by loud teenagers and their litter.

Notes

[1] See *Lifetime Learning* (DfEE, 1995); *The Learning Age* (DfEE, 1998) and *Realising the Potential* (Foster, 2005).

[2] Lave and Wenger offer a social theory of learning in which the learning process concerns social participation rather than the acquisition of knowledge by individuals. The link between learning and identity has important implications for transforming not only the individual but the community of learning and the wider community of influence of that individual.

[3] Student expectations and comments on their experiences can be found in the National Student Survey carried out by the LSC (see www.lsc.gov.uk).

[4] See the Lifelong Learning UK website: www.lifelonglearninguk.org

2 A curriculum for work and life

In this chapter we will consider the policy priorities that have shaped and continue to shape the curriculum for adult learners.[1] In particular, we will look at the tensions between learning for social and for economic purposes as defined by governments and by students themselves, which we as practitioners have to manage on the ground. *Teaching the FE Curriculum* by Mark Weyers deals with curriculum planning in more depth. My intention here is to set a historical context and draw out key themes that can be identified in contemporary educational discourses, in order to help us engage with current debates about the content and funding of opportunities for adults. We will then discuss some national and local developments which seek to provide a curriculum that better meets the needs of employers and offers a flexible approach to learning which takes more account of the experience and needs of the learner.

So what is the purpose of education for adults?

In the nineteenth century, industrialization required a very different workforce from pre-industrial society. This workforce needed to be educated sufficiently to read instructions related to the new machinery and industrial processes and thus become effective employees.

The downside of the growth of the 'urban' industrial economy was poverty, slums, poor working conditions, sickness and crime, which caused public concern. This led to political intervention in the form of the Poor Laws and state elementary and technical education for 'the mental and moral improvement' of the working classes.

The late nineteenth century saw a huge expansion of technical education, often in evening schools, which is interesting in the current context of 14–19 education, in that they catered for adolescents (15 plus) as well as adults (17 plus). The curriculum was low-level technical and craft education, together with the 'three Rs' and practical 'domestic' courses for women, plus some moral instruction and recreational provision.[2]

From this period onwards, we can see the twin concerns of economic and social reform at the heart of government education policy, together with an ongoing debate about the extent to which the cost of adult education, especially that which does not have a direct vocational purpose, should be met by public funds.

Post-war education provision for adults

The 1944 Education Act gave LEAs the duty of securing efficient primary, secondary and further education in their areas. The primary purpose of this newly named 'further education' was preparation for work, and it was deemed to include full- and part-time education for people over compulsory school age and, interestingly, 'leisure-time occupation ... for any persons ... able and willing to profit by the facilities provided for that purpose'. In addition, institutions also had to provide 'organised cultural training and recreation activities' (Education Act 1944: clause 41). We can deduce from this that the aim of the Act was to create greater equality of opportunities within a meritocratic society rather than to use FE as a tool for radical social reform.

In the 1950s and 1960s, British FE began to outgrow its narrow technical and vocational confines and to embrace the full spectrum of adult learning. Britain had been the only country in Europe to make a distinction between vocational and predominantly non-vocational education.

The 1973 oil crisis, rising inflation, the long-term decline in Britain's manufacturing industries and the consequent rise in unemployment resulted in government pressure for adult education to take on a more directly vocational role, in the hope that this would contribute to economic recovery. A growing concern was that the economic crisis disproportionately affected the white and minority ethnic working classes, and there was a rise in poverty, homelessness and crime in inner cities and an increase in the number of people depending on state benefits. The response of the Thatcher government was to try to stimulate an enterprise culture and return to Victorian values of 'self help' and thrift. Education was a tool to bring about the desired social change. In the 1980s the Conservative government set up a succession of 'training agencies'. These new funding streams increased central control of the content and process of education and training while helping to conceal rising unemployment figures. With these funds FE colleges set up new daytime provision aimed at addressing youth and adult unemployment.[3]

The 1992 Further and Higher Education Act presented a vision of a 'new education' that would inspire and sustain economic growth, and promoted the progression of market values in the public sector – competition, efficiency and value for money, together with the notion of student choice and the raising of standards. Through it, the government attempted to bridge the academic/vocational divide, raise the status of vocational courses and supply a suitably trained and skilled workforce.

The Act gave adults, for the first time, a statutory right to publicly funded education. Government pressure on higher and further education institutions to expand resulted in a significant increase in the number of mature students. By 1994 approximately three-quarters of FE students were adults and a significant number, including a growing proportion of people from minority ethnic groups, were progressing to higher education.[4]

Vocational courses leading to qualifications were mostly delivered through FE colleges and funded through the Further Education Funding Council (FEFC). Meanwhile, local authorities were given the responsibility to provide other forms of adult learning with a growing brief to engage socially excluded groups who had few or no qualifications, as a first step to enable them to gain employment.

In order to ensure that the 'new FE' was forced into working more closely with industry, a number of new initiatives and mechanisms were put into place. Colleges were required to compete with each other to bid to the Training and Enterprise Councils (TECs) for funding.[5] National Targets for Education and Training (NTETs) were set, National Vocational Qualifications (NVQs) were launched, with standards set by industry, and the Department for Education and Employment (DfEE) was created, placing employment at the heart of publicly funded post-school education.

In the 1990s, government policy statements highlighted the value of learning throughout adulthood.[6] In the 2000s, it is clear that an increasing proportion of the cost of adult provision (especially of 'leisure' learning) will need to be met by the learner or their employer. The purpose and value of educating adults remains much as it was defined in the nineteenth century. The question of the control of what is taught and who should pay for it remains contested.

The learning and skills sector

The Learning and Skills Council (LSC) was founded in 2000 to ensure not only that government policy is implemented, but also that it has an impact. It has responsibility for all publicly-funded post-16 education and training delivered outside higher education establishments. The three priorities for the sector are familiar: first, a need to develop industrial training to increase Britain's skill base in order to develop the nation's economic competitive strength; second, a need to widen participation in education by people who have few, or no formal qualifications, in order to get them into employment and not dependent on welfare payments; and third, the need to find strategies that encourage social inclusion and reduce crime.

Adults in the learning and skills sector

- 14% of adults of working age have no qualifications (Foster Report).
- 40% of adults in the workforce lack a basic level 2 qualification – 5 GCSEs A–C or equivalent (LSC).
- 5 million adults have literacy and numeracy skills below level 1 (Foster Report).
- 25–30% of adults have undertaken no formal learning since leaving school (NALS).
- More than 3.5 million adults are enrolled on learning programmes to improve their skills.
- Approximately 2.35 million students are enrolled in FE colleges, of whom 73% are over 19. They are studying 1.2 qualifications each (ILR 2002–3).
- 61% of adults in FE are female and 39% are male (ILR).
- 14% of adults in FE are non-white (ILR)
- Since 1996, the number of adults engaged in FE has dropped from 40% to 38% and participation by people in social groups D and E has dropped from 26% to 23% (Aldridge and Tuckett 2004).
- Education and training is provided by:
  420 FE colleges
  150 LEAs
  35 independent external institutions
  14 specialist designated institutions, including the WEA (ALI).
- The split of LSC-funded adult learners by type of provider is (LSC 2004):
  73% FE
  23% adult and community learning
  4% work-based learning.
- The level of study on LSC-funded courses is (LSC 2004):
  3% level 4 and above
  26% level 3
  31% level 2
  40% below level 2.

A curriculum for the learning and skills sector

Given the complexity of the sector, how can we minimize duplication and fill gaps in provision to create a coherent, flexible and relevant curriculum? More importantly, how can we facilitate student progression between different levels and different providers so learners can build up learning credit over time? At a strategic level the restructured LSC has a key planning role, given impetus by the Foster Report (2005). However, we all need to contribute to local curriculum initiatives to ensure that they are workable in practice and actually meet the needs of employers and our communities.

Flexible programming and the National Credit Framework

Programmes that will attract and retain adult students need to be compatible with the patterns of adult lives and provide modes of attendance which include short courses and modular programmes, so that students can take a 'learning break', move from one course to another, or leave a course early to start a job.[7]

If you talk to anyone about their own learning since they left school, it is likely to be more like crazy paving than a career ladder. A typical example might include: learning a language, learning to drive and first aid training. Any of these could be vocationally related or for personal interest; they could be provided by an employer, LSC-funded organization, or a private trainer. So how useful is it to try to define what is 'vocational' and what is 'personal interest' learning? It is clear that 'learning for work and life are inseparable' (Hughes 2005). Can we have one system that embraces all adult learning?

In recent years, a number of flexible models have been advanced, including modularization and open or distance learning and, more recently, e-learning (see *ICT and e-Learning* by Whalley et al.).[8] Many community organizations offer 'roll-on, roll-off' programmes, often with Open College Network (OCN) accreditation. The challenge is to offer flexibility rather than fragmentation: students who are neither competent nor confident learners require an anchor (that is, *us*) to help them maintain focus and momentum. One way of doing this is through a national credit framework.

Since 2004, the Qualifications and Curriculum Authority (QCA) has been drawing on developments by institutions and OCNs in order to achieve the National Qualifications Framework (NQF). This will provide pathways (or perhaps a climbing frame) that allows people to earn, use and bank credit[9] in bite-sized chunks throughout their lives. The development of credit systems for learning and skills is usefully discussed by Tait (2003), and the QCA framework is described in its consultation document, *A Framework for Achievement* (QCA 2004), though it is beyond the scope of this book to go into details here.

Curriculum innovation

Much of what is offered to adults in FE is 'tried and tested' qualifications, such as those accredited by City and Guilds and Edexcel, along with some locally-devised OCN courses. On the ground, we have had to respond to a plethora of initiatives focused on widening participation, raising standards and increasing success rates. Some developmental provisions, such as the Adult Community Learning Fund, have supported innovation, but in general the focus on targets and short-term project funding has meant that there is very little slack to try new curriculum approaches.[10] We need actively to seek ways to make our curriculum content and delivery more dynamic and relevant if we are successfully to engage people from traditional non-participant backgrounds, and those in a long-term unemployment situation such as ex-offenders who currently do not believe that education has anything to offer them. In Chapter 4, we will look at some successful curriculum strategies employed by FE and ACL providers that widen participation and are linked into progression pathways.

Vocational education

Defining 'vocational education' is not as easy as one might suppose. The end of 'jobs for life', 'globalization' and developments in information technology mean that the boundaries between home and work are blurred and we all need to be prepared to change our jobs several times during an increasingly long working life. We may even want to make a total career change from one occupation to another, or turn a leisure interest into paid employment. Perhaps the key vocational skill we should be teaching adults is the ability to cope with continuous uncertainty and change.

FE has historically been seen by government as a key way to deliver education and training to enable an individual to gain competence in their occupational area and thus contribute to the economy. Current policy initiatives focus on shifting people of working age out of welfare and into employment, and on addressing the effects of globalization and technological innovation. Recent LSRC research (Stasz and Wright 2004) makes it clear that Britain does not have what could be described as a vocational education 'system' within or beyond FE. Stasz and Wright state that the overall inadequacy of data on training places available, and on the people enrolled on vocational courses or requiring training, makes effective human resource planning by employers, especially small and medium-sized enterprises (SMEs), difficult. This lack of good information then makes it hard for employers to articulate what they want from a vocational education system. Despite restructuring, the sector remains complex. The Foster Report calls for 'relentless streamlining of qualifications and learning pathways' to make provision more 'user-friendly' (Foster 2005:7). There are 115 QCA-approved awarding bodies and 5,356 qualifications within the NQF, with thousands of other awarding bodies and qualifications that are not recognized.[11] However, not all qualifications are available to everybody and some serve a particular niche market. 'Appropriateness' and 'choice' are key issues.

Employers and the learning and skills sector

550,000 vocational qualifications go into the nation's labour force from colleges every year (AOC).
The average college helps 500 local companies to upskill every year (AOC).

Funding sources

- DfES
- LSC
- Department for Work and Pensions
- Regional Development Agencies
- Office of the Deputy Prime Minister
- employers
- European Social Fund

Institutions providing services through classroom and worksite instruction

- FE colleges
- workplaces
- community organizations, including Ufi/Learndirect hubs
- private training providers
- prisons

Key vocational targets

- Increase participation in higher education, towards 50% of those aged 18–30 by 2010.
- Improve the basic skills levels of 1.5 million adults by 2007.
- Reduce by 40% the number of adults in the workforce who lack NVQ level 2 or equivalent by 2010.

Recent government initiatives to promote vocational learning

The aims of government are to encourage people to gain and update vocational skills, to make FE more responsive to employers, and also to get employers to make a greater financial contribution to training. It is doing this through a variety of 'carrot and stick' measures: Centres of Vocational Excellence (COVE) 'badging' rewards colleges with strong vocational links and good quality provision; apprenticeships have been re-invented, with the aim of raising the proportion of adult workers who have at least a level 2 qualification; Train to Gain (T2G)[12] offers employers a skills brokerage service and subsidized free training; finally, twelve new Skills Academies are to be created. These will be linked to the industries in which they specialize via the network of newly created Sector Skills Councils, which set training standards in each industry and act as the voice of employers in vocational education policy-making. Provision that does not support government priorities will not be funded.

If you work in a college, your institution will need to respond to local, as well as national, priorities, including employer engagement (EE) targets set by the local LSC. There are obviously great differences in the way that FE works with employers in areas where there are large companies involved in manufacturing, in rural areas and in those areas with a majority of service industries or SMEs. In addition to customized training for employees, types of employer involvement include: employers acting as a professional client and setting 'live projects'; pro-viding work experience placements; and mentoring students. Employers are also members of college corporations and some adult students may also be, or may become, employers.[13]

The range is so great and some of the issues so knotty, this topic could be a book on its own. So in what follows, I have identified some of the key issues that can be applied in most situations.

Why learning work skills is important for adults

No assumptions should be made about adult students' previous experience, skills or confidence in any situation; this includes employment. There are many reasons why adults may not have had a positive or recent experience of paid employment. These may include redundancy, accident or illness (including mental health problems), or a period in prison. Women, and sometimes men, may have taken a break from paid employment to look after children or elderly or sick relations. Some people may never have had paid employment. There are adults who have been educated and worked abroad who may need to update vocational skills and achieve a British qualification, improve their English, or gain an understanding of the culture of British organizations in order to gain suitable employment. Students who have been recently employed may want to make a career change and need to gain knowledge of a different profession or industry, or may be seeking a promotion for which they need a different set of skills. Every student will have his or her own set of needs beyond vocational skills, such as adjusting to going out to work every day, or accepting the additional responsibility that promotion brings.

How to make vocational learning attractive to adult students

Adult students have *chosen* to be in our class – always a good start! We are experts in our subjects and should have kept up to date with new skills and knowledge of our 'industry'. In FE, there have traditionally been a lot of part-time staff who are currently employed in their specialisms, and students really like being taught by a chef from a high-class local restaurant or being instructed in gilding skills by the head of conservation at the museum. They are learning an insider's 'tricks of the trade' and making professional contacts. It is therefore unsurprising that Walhberg and Gleeson's (2003) research describes the negative effect on learning of a business studies course with no work experience and no clear progression into employment. It may be that in your subject, students undertake placements or you get visiting speakers – the possibilities for industry links are numerous and the key message is to 'make learning relevant'. Don't forget that it is not all one way. In my own college, staff are members of advisory committees, deliver in-service training and provide consultancies to local businesses.

The very best situations for staff, employers and the local community are those in which courses are planned and taught collaboratively. Initial work in these areas can often be funded as a project, e.g. regeneration funding. Use your imagination and your professional contacts and get out of the classroom. Just because it is not being done does not mean that it cannot be done and possibly should be done. *Breaking Down the Barriers* (Champney *et al.* 2005) provides a toolkit of successful widening participation strategies. The example in the box below outlines how one college matched a local employer's needs with the learning needs of its community to benefit both.

Employment projects in health and care at Kensington and Chelsea College

The start of these developments was the NHS and Social Care sector requiring more staff and also requiring training for employees. Eighty per cent of employees in social care do not have a qualification relevant to their work. Every aspect of the course was devised and is delivered in partnership. Students are recruited through community 'road shows' run by the FE/NHS partnership.

Realising the Potential, level 1 basic skills in care with English support

Aims: getting hard-to-reach learners involved in education and training and informing them of the breadth of employment opportunities available in the health service.

Progression pathway: Pre-Access (ESOL) or ASET Certificate in care practice (level 2); access to nursing, occupational therapy (level 3).

Partners: Primary Care Trust and LSC.

Essence of Care (Health Care Assistants), level 1

Aims: to recruit new staff with more diverse backgrounds from the local community and develop existing hospital employees so they have improved skills and career prospects.

Partner: Local Hospital Trust.

The course is a rolling programme of nine OCN units at level 1, delivered jointly by the college and hospital over

---

five weeks. Students have an induction programme, classroom work, workplace practical, private study and two tutorials. They receive a course handbook, workbook and work experience diary. The target group is minority ethnic students whose first language is not English, so basic skills support is available.

In 2004/2005 the programme had 91% completion and achievement across the five courses. A level 2 course is now being developed.

Strategies to engage new adult learners

• Start where the students are, e.g. in the community.
• Provide first-step learning in non-institutional buildings.
• Link training with real jobs and where possible have employer involvement.
• Design the curriculum as part of a progression pathway with different points of entry and exit.
• Break the curriculum into small steps with accreditation at each stage.
• Integrate skills for life and IT with vocational learning.
• Develop an active partnership with the voluntary sector.

Workplace cultures as danger zones[14]

Students taking vocational courses that offer a real experience of the workplace and potential employment at the end of the course may experience tensions caused by the culture in the workplace. The Transforming Learning Cultures in Further Education project concluded that, as a result of the close and synergistic links with employers in some vocational areas such as childcare, there is a strong integration of college and workplace learning and very effective preparation for employment in this field. As part of this research, Colley *et al.* (2003) found that the relationship between learning and identity results in 'learning as becoming'. Therefore a student does not merely learn photography, engineering or healthcare: he or she becomes a photographer, engineer or nurse. This 'becoming' should be mostly a positive experience that raises self-esteem.

However, this research also identified a downside, which is that the maintenance of traditional workplace values and practices is not always a good thing. Adult students in particular may find it difficult to adjust their own behaviours. Indeed, in some situations, it may not be reasonable that they do. For example, it could mean that women learning to become professional carers are also learning to accept low wages, and men training for some male-dominated industries are also being trained to continue established macho behaviour.

We need to reflect on our own behaviour. To what extent are we enculturated into vocational norms? Do we question the practices and culture of our own specialist areas? It has obviously worked for us. We would, of course, challenge overt discrimination in a placement, but workplace cultures can be more subtle. Are we unwittingly providing an education that teaches students how to fit into a culture that challenges their sense of identity? What opportunities do we give them to discuss their vocational experiences and their feelings about such experiences? Does this conflict with encouraging students to have aspirations and confidence in their own ideas and opinions that may result in them challenging 'norms'?

Enculturation is a complex process and students are not without power or choice. Unfortunately, the choice may be to reject the experience rather than seek to challenge it (see Chapter 6). We cannot change the world, or even our industry, but we owe it to ourselves and our students to reflect on whose values are privileged in our interactions with students and employers and if necessary find allies with whom we can work to change things we do not like.

I've changed my mind!

It is perfectly reasonable for a student's vocational aspirations to alter as a result of engaging in learning (it is not necessarily a 'failure' of our information, advice and guidance services). This may mean that after the end of the course they decide that they do not want to work in the area they have studied. If we maintain a broad view of learning, we can focus on the trans-ferability of skills that a student has acquired, such as research and communication skills, rather than see their change of direction as a failure by them, or ourselves. Colley *et al.* (2003) found that in courses where there is a strong vocational culture, a student's change of aspiration resulted in them being socially 'cut adrift' through the behaviour of other students and staff. We are there to enable a release from, not add to, personal histories of failure. It is also important to have a broad definition of 'work', for example, unwaged labour in the home is work! Acting as a volunteer for a while can be a more useful step to build a career than doing a dead-end job. Some of our students do all of these things as well as study. Our job is to help them make the different experiences count in building a career, or even a second career.

Delivering the curriculum dream

There are contradictions and inconsistencies in government policy. As managers and lecturers, it is our actions, through putting policy into practice, that reveal the tensions and indeed contest some ideas or initiatives. The twin goals of raising the skills of the population and achieving social justice are not always easy to achieve, for example: one current challenge is to find ways to ensure that people with few qualifications, or who are on low incomes, are able to access the full curriculum, not merely an instrumental one of basic skills and low-level vocational qualifications.

As previously discussed, an additional complication in curriculum planning is that adult students define their own learning aims within what is offered, so that categorizing provision into 'vocational' and 'leisure' is problematic. Is having a group of students with different life experiences and different learning goals a problem? Not for the learners, in fact the social mix that results from a 'comprehensive' intake adds to the learning experience. It can, however, be a problem for providers, for example if students enrol for courses leading to qualifications, but do not take the examination, as this adversely affects success rates.

The challenge to educators is to meet government targets while providing a curriculum that offers equal and real choices to all social groups. In the chapters that follow we will look more closely at the factors that threaten, or help realize, the dream that engagement in adult learning can bring about positive personal, economic and social change.

Notes

[1] Yvonne Hillier's book in the managers' series, *Everything You Need To Know about FE Policy*, deals with policy in more depth.

[2] This echoes current priorities for adults in FE – *Skills for Life* and a full level 2 qualification.

[3] See Kelly (1992) and Fieldhouse (1998) for more information on youth training schemes and programmes to re-engage adults, including Fresh Horizons and Wider Opportunities for Women.

[4] The FEFC Chief Inspector's report for 1994–95.

[5] TECs were quangos with boards of directors dominated by representatives of local business to promote work-relevant education and training in FE.

[6] By the Conservatives in *Lifetime Learning* (DfEE 1995) and by Labour in *The Learning Age* (DfEE 1998)

[7] See Foster (2005), page 7.

[8] See the DfES e-learning strategy (www.dfes.gov.uk/publications/e-strategy) and also BECTA's work in the aclearn pages for adult and community (www.aclearn.net/display.cfm?page=938).

[9] Credit: an award made to someone in recognition of the verified achievement of designated learning outcomes at a specified level.

[10] ALI inspector Richard Moore, speaking at a conference on adult learning (CLLP, London, May 2005), stated that inspections had found that innovative provision was often not sustainable due to funding constraints.

[11] Source: QCA, January 2006.

[12] Train to Gain is an LSC service for businesses. It provides a free brokerage service that matches their business needs with training providers and ensures relevant, high quality delivery. The service is prompted by the significant skills shortages that continue to have a negative impact on UK productivity and competitiveness.

[13] We need to avoid the stereotype of an 'employer'. This could be a parent wanting childcare, or the owner of a hair salon – don't just think Alan Sugar or Richard Branson!

[14] The vocational curriculum is not neutral. It is a product of relations of power. A useful theoretical approach to understanding this is provided by Bourdieu, in particular his concept of 'field'.

3 Promoting equality and diversity

The highly influential Kennedy Report on widening participation in education and training made it clear that the economic success of the UK and many other countries:

> will depend upon maximising the potential of all. Drawing upon the talents of an educational elite, or even an educated majority, will not be enough. Social cohesion will only be achieved if the capacity of everyone to contribute to and benefit from the social, cultural and personal dimensions of their lives is developed through learning. (FEFC 1997: 4)

While there are two books in this series that deal in depth with this subject (*A Guide to Diversity in FE* by Colquhoun *et al.* and *A Guide to Race Equality* by Ainley), it is important that there is some discussion here in relation to adult learning.

The widening participation and social justice agendas

Numerous studies have revealed that the majority of adults who participate in education and training are those from higher socio-economic groups. As a result, successive governments have required FE to be more effective in widening participation. This has been driven in part by notions of equity and fairness, but also by economics.[1] Key studies, the most important of which was the Kennedy Report (FEFC 1997a) have determined policy.[2] More recently, the McPherson Inquiry (1999) into the death of Stephen Lawrence made a number of recommendations specifically aimed at both challenging racism and promoting cultural diversity. These recommendations were made with the statutory education system in mind, but have a direct bearing on and applicability to the education of adults.

Colleges and other organizations have been encouraged to develop practices that aim to promote equality of opportunity to ensure that, as far as possible, groups and individuals who are educationally, socially and economically disadvantaged have the same opportunities for success as other groups of the population. Colleges have been supported in tackling social exclusion through a number of initiatives, including Inclusive Learning[3] and Skills for Life. Learner support funds have been made available to help poorer students pay for childcare, travel, books and equipment. The LSC requires colleges to set equality and diversity targets and to evaluate the impact of their policies on practice through the annual Self Assessment Report. This is monitored by inspection.[4]

As a result, a great deal has been done, especially in relation to publicity, physical access, learning support and basic skills awareness: but education and training has to appear relevant to an individual's life, and there are still large numbers of people with low qualifications who do not think that education has anything positive to offer them. Benn (1998) suggests that this is because many adult education providers still believe that offering the same curriculum to all students will result in an equivalence of outcome. This fails to recognize that men and women of different ages, classes and race do not receive teaching in the same set of circumstances.

There remain major issues that need to be addressed; in particular, the content and delivery of the curriculum and the way success is measured. These aspects still protect the interests of the dominant majority. For example, in order for students to be successful in a course, it may be necessary for them to become enculturated into the values and practices of the profession(s) linked to it. This may be undesirable, for example if it supports gender stereotyping and low pay. It is up to us to change the culture. At my own college, for example, we are working with athletes who are disabled to develop new modules and learning materials on our vocational sports courses.

It is therefore clear that policies and course opportunities alone are not enough. Education has to be part of a long-term project to shift the social inequalities that exist in society, to raise aspirations and contribute to social cohesion. This may sound daunting, but there are actions that we can take as individuals that will make a difference, and collectively there is even more possibility of change.

Institutionalized prejudice including racism and sexism

It is important that we learn to recognize the discourses[5] in society and embedded in the education system[6] that limit the choices and opportunities available to people from particular groups, including women, members of ethnic communities and people with disabilities. Because they have developed over time and often appear as 'common sense', they are difficult to address by the individual lecturer, but we need to recognize their presence as this impacts on every aspect of college life, from the paucity of black and minority ethnic staff[7] and people with disabilities in senior management, to curriculum and assessment techniques that may disadvantage certain groups.

In order to promote equality effectively, we need to be constantly aware of our own history and social positioning and reflect critically on how we select students for our courses and interact with them in the class or the workplace. As lecturers and managers, we need to keep learning and to be involved in a continuous process of discovery and interpretation. We need to work actively to bring about positive change at an individual student and wider institutional level.

Social structures affect the way students, or potential students, react to the curriculum offer that is made to them. A significant number of adults who do not see formal education as relevant to their lives:[8] this may be because initial education has not left them feeling valued, which, together with their wider life experience, creates a complex inter-relationship between feelings about educational establishments and their own self-esteem:[9]

When educational disadvantage is compounded by other material differences – of gender, ethnicity, poverty, class, disability and sexuality – the effect is often a denial of imagined possibility. (O'Rourke 1995: 111)

We need to find ways to make educational provision relevant to learners, help them build skills and confidence and aspire to achieve their full potential, by opening up new possibilities to them.

Diversity Statistics

- 29% of learners in general FE come from the 25% poorest postcodes.
- 16% of students in FE are non-white ethnic as against 8% in the population as a whole.
- Participation rates in higher education by lower social groups has not increased despite government interventions (HESA 2003).
- 27% of higher education entrants from FE Access courses are from minority ethnic groups, as against 17% of all other entrants (HESA 2005).
- 75% of Access students are women.
- 50% of disabled people of working age are unemployed (DRC survey).
- 8.48% (305,494) adult students declared a disability (LSC 2004), which reflects the proportion in the population.
- 5.5% of Access to higher education students declared a disability (2004).

Reflecting on our own practice

First, ensure that you are familiar with current policies and procedures regarding equality and diversity in your organization. These will clearly state your role and responsibilities for dealing with direct and indirect discrimination and promoting equality of opportunity. They should also identify who can provide you with further information and support.

Direct discrimination

This occurs when a person is treated less favourably than another simply because of a personal characteristic.

Indirect discrimination

This occurs when a policy or requirement, which at first glance seems fair, in fact operates to the detriment of a particular group of people because of a characteristic of that group, such as age, family circumstances or gender, and the requirement is not reasonable or necessary in the circumstances.

We must constantly reflect on our own attitudes to and knowledge about the people we teach. Do we know enough about them as individuals? Do we recognize and value their differences? What expectations do we have of them and how is this communicated by our behaviour? For example, do we instinctively ask women students to look after someone who seems upset or to organize social events? Do we see a forceful woman as 'bossy' but a forceful man as 'commanding' and treat them accordingly? Do we always ensure a wide variety of images that challenge social stereotypes? Do we give adequate notice of assignments so that lone parents and people with care commitments can fit them around their domestic responsibilities? Do we make adequate checks that educational visits and work experience placements can cater for the needs of students with disabilities in a positive and dignified way? Even our best endeavours can be let down by the poor practice of others, as exemplified by the experiences of an art lecturer:

> I took my students to a national art collection in London. I checked on accessibility, as I have a student in a wheelchair. When we arrived, there were entrance steps. The doorman did not know where the wheelchair accessible entrance was. When I found it, it was round the back of the building and the lift was out of order. The student insisted on making his own way up the steps on his hands and knees and I took his wheelchair up.

Whatever subject we teach, we can find ways to draw on the diversity of cultures and the skills and knowledge that our students have; to challenge them to look beyond their own experiences and have confidence that they can achieve. For example, older people can learn new things, and women can be successful in traditional male occupational areas, but we need to help them acquire strategies and confidence to deal with ageism or 'laddish' cultures in the workplace (James and Diment 2003). The expectations that we have of students and their aspirations should be based on them as individuals, not as members of a particular community. However, we need to recognize that they operate in different spheres in which they will encounter discrimination and that some people experience multiple disadvantage or prejudice because they are seen, for example, as black and gay or old and female.

Colleges strive to ensure that their literature and the images associated with their college activities reflect the balance of the communities they serve and fairly represent all relevant groups. Despite the emphasis on equality and diversity, it is not always easy to find commercially produced visual materials that present appropriate and positive messages about all social groups and are adult-focused. This may mean producing your own materials. For example, the textbooks available for some modern foreign languages do not challenge gender stereotypes, include a range of ethnic groups or provide positive images of people with disabilities. Yet if you teach a language such as French, it is easy to find images and texts about other parts of the world where French is spoken, rather than limit your content to France; or you may be able to use materials designed for another subject area, such as English for Speakers of Other Languages (ESOL).

Education is more than acquiring a narrow range of technical skills; it is about enrichment, cultural understanding and social cohesion too. We must ensure that the course learning objectives reflect this; it should be made explicit so that we can evaluate the effectiveness of our practice.

Dealing with differences and commonalties between students and social groups

By trying to treat everyone the same and by not understanding and responding to the different social positions of students, our actions imply a 'neutrality', but we are in fact unwittingly supporting the interests of dominant groups, i.e. white, male, able-bodied, middle class, heterosexual. We should recognize and value differences between people and employ strategies that help people to empower themselves and challenge discrimination.

Not all members of one social group experience life in the same way, and generalizations about, say, women or Muslim students imply a unitary experience, which is far from the reality. Yet there are instances when the combined needs of women as mothers or Muslim students during Ramadan may be important to recognize at a policy level. Shared experiences are important, as this creates the possibility of empowerment and political agency. We therefore have to find ways to recognize the differences between individuals without ending up with fragmentation, which weakens the argument for educational policy linked to social policy.

We need to be aware of the inter-relationship of differences, for example white working-class and middle-class women experience patriarchal relationships differently and their social class experiences also place them in differential power relationships with each other. This can be further fractured by ethnicity, able-bodiedness, sexuality and so on. So, while identifying differences can result in some groups becoming 'the other', 'outsiders', so finding commonalties can result in 'the accumulation of oppressed identities' (Maynard, 1994: 19). In order to widen participation, we are therefore asked to work with 'the homeless' or 'the unemployed' but we need to ensure that in the learning environment, be it a college classroom, community venue, or prison, we give each student an individualized experience that 'levels the playing-field' and promotes equality of opportunity.

In Chapter 1, I emphasized the need to recognize adult students' prior learning and relevant life experiences. However, we must always remember that disclosure of personal information has consequences for the individual, and identifying difference can feel uncomfortable and even damage self-esteem or classroom relationships. We need to be aware of our own power relationship with our students. For example, Afshar (1994: 136) has described the importance of privacy in family matters and loyalty to one's husband, in relation to expectations of the behaviour of Muslim women. She says that Islam defines a woman as dependent on men thus: 'any transgression denotes a failure not only of the women, but also and particularly of their menfolk and hence the entire family' (Afshar, 1994: 134). Disclosure of personal matters is therefore not only a breach of privacy, but also has the potential to bring shame on the whole family. Allan (1990) and Finch (1983) have argued that for some members of the working class, 'privacy' may also be linked with notions of 'respectability'. For black students, privacy concerning their families may be an attempt to deny information which leads to pathologizing the behaviour of black families (Phoenix 1987).

So while, for example, holding a group discussion on a childcare course that draws on students' experience of child-rearing practices in their own cultures can be an excellent way of valuing difference and of supporting respectful relationships with parents in the nursery, we need to be vigilant that it does not have the opposite effect and feed personal prejudices or 'normalizing' notions of the family. Also, the way something is intended is not always the way it is received. We must be careful that a genuine wish to learn from and understand our students does not appear to them to be, for example, a way to elicit sympathy inappropriately in the case of a student with a physical disability, or to 'exoticize' another culture in a way that may be perceived as being subtly patronizing or discriminatory.

We need to be clear about what will be gained through discussing differences and remember that the 'unquestioning celebration' of differences in classrooms does little to change women's relationships with men, racial prejudice or other forms of discrimination.

Race

Race – legal requirements of colleges

Under the Race Relations Act 1976 as amended by the Race Relations (Amendment) Act 2000, colleges have the following general duties:

- eliminate unlawful race discrimination
- promote equality of opportunity
- promote good relations between people from different racial groups.

As a result of the McPherson Report and recent legislation, all education providers are now expected to examine the effectiveness of their practices and procedures in the areas of recruiting, retaining, teaching and raising the achievements of adults and young people from black and minority groups.

Colleges also have the following specific duties:

- to prepare a written statement of the policy for promoting race equality
- to put in place arrangements for implementing the policy, publicizing its contents and the results of monitoring its effectiveness
- to assess the impact of its policies on learners and staff of different racial groups
- to monitor, by reference to those racial groups, the admission and progress of learners and the recruitment and career progress of staff.

Gender[10]

Women have traditionally made good use of local education services for adults. A key factor influencing their involvement has always been whether learning could be fitted around their domestic and work commitments. Education has provided some women not only with skills and knowledge, but with personal space.

A broad range of women now study in the learning and skills sector, and more than ever before are achieving qualifications. It is therefore disappointing that statistics reveal that irrespective of qualification (from none to degree), men's gross weekly earnings are still higher than those of women. This is often because women gravitate towards traditional female areas of study and employment, which have lower status, and because they have career breaks to look after children. However, we should not see what we do in a totally negative way. FE does give women from a variety of backgrounds the opportunity to convert 'caring' skills, traditionally used in the home, into accredited professional skills as nurses, hairdressers, social workers or counsellors: occupational roles that bring with them status and economic independence.

Teaching students with disabilities or learning difficulties

Disability – legal requirements of colleges

Under the Disability Discrimination Act Part 4, colleges have the following duties.

- To ensure that someone is not treated less favourably than someone else for a reason related to his or her disability, without justification.
- To take reasonable steps to find out if a person has a disability and act accordingly.
- To anticipate the kind of adjustments that disabled students might need to allow them to access services.
- To treat information about an individual's disability appropriately in line with the student's wish for confidentiality and the Data Protection Act.
- To take responsibility for informing all relevant staff once a student has disclosed a disability and agrees that the information can be passed on.
- To actively promote disability equality (from December 2006).

It is important that, from the first contact, students who have a disability or learning difficulty are reassured that everyone in the college will do their best to make adjustments and support them in their learning. However, it is understandable that not all students with disabilities notify the college when they apply, for fear of not being accepted. We therefore have to create the right atmosphere at every stage of their engagement so that they feel confident to disclose a disability and are reassured that this will not lead to them being discriminated against in any way. If someone tells you about a disability or learning difficulty that they have not previously revealed to anyone in the college, you need to follow local procedures for confidentiality and disclosure to ensure that appropriate adjustments are made and that support is provided without breaking trust. If they insist on the information remaining confidential, this should be respected, but the student needs to know that this may mean that the college will not be able to meet all their learning needs.

We are not expected to have detailed knowledge about all types of disability and learning difficulty. What we do need to know is who in our organization can support us with appropriate teaching strategies, assistive technology, communication support for students with sensory impairments or other disabilities, or can refer us to best practice elsewhere. We need to discuss expectations and course requirements to avoid problems arising over time. Sometimes a student will need to be referred to a more appropriate course or provider, but we must be clear that this is for sound academic reasons.

Mental health – government policy

The Mental Health and Social Exclusion Report (Social Exclusion Unit 2004) aims to: modernize mental health services so that people experiencing mental health difficulties will be supported to access mainstream services; tackle stigma and discrimination by supporting the social inclusion of people with mental health difficulties; challenge the culture of low expectations placed upon people with mental health difficulties; and support achievement and success. The report's performance indicators for education are to increase the number of adults with mental health difficulties achieving level 2 qualifications, and to increase the number of adults on Care Programme Approach accessing mainstream education.

Whereas students transferring from school are likely to bring records with them, or have their application endorsed by a reference from a member of staff, it is not standard practice to ask adult students for personal information about their health, or for a reference (unless they are going to work in a vocational area such as health or care where they may be asked for a reference and a certificate from the Criminal Record Bureau). There is a social stigma attached to mental ill health, so a student may not inform us about his or her condition. There may also be instances when a student is not aware that he or she is ill. Teaching students with poor mental health is fine if they are taking prescribed medication and it is effective, but if the condition is not under control, mental health problems can manifest themselves as challenging behaviour. This can be distressing for the individual and can disrupt learning for the rest of the class. Always get advice and support from college managers about the best way to handle the situation, as with swift action the student can be supported appropriately and the class ethos maintained. Remember that positive adult learning opportunities may be of particular benefit to students with mental health problems. Your class may have great value for these students. They may need additional support and sensitive understanding, and it is particularly important to treat these students equitably, fairly and compassionately.

The most knowledgeable person to talk to about how best to support the learning of someone with a disability is nearly always the student him or herself. It is important that we allow students to express their needs and that we respond appropriately.

Ways we can help students with disabilities in the classroom

(See Appendix II for details of some useful organizations.)

General

- Treat learners as individuals, not conditions, and focus on their abilities.
- Don't assume we know what the implications of a disability are; ask the learners themselves – they are the experts on the effects of their learning difficulty or disability.
- Be aware of our own attitude (e.g. pity or embarrassment). It is usually our attitude, rather than the learner's disability, that creates barriers.
- Carry out a risk assessment and ensure that key people, including other students in the class, know what to do in the case of emergency evacuation.

Deafness or other hearing impairments

- Remember that a deaf person cannot lipread/watch an interpreter at the same time as reading other materials. Give deaf learners time to read notes/handouts.
- Ask the student (discreetly) if he or she would benefit from sitting at the front of the class. Use the whiteboard to write down your main topics. This will help learners to catch the flow when you are giving a lecture/presentation.
- Stand in good light to help lipreading.
- Use a hearing loop for hearing aid users.
- Provide a sign language interpreter or communication support worker (CSW) and ensure you allow breaks for them.
- When using an interpreter or CSW, address the deaf learner and not the interpreter or CSW.
- Ensure there are good acoustics for learners with hearing difficulties and that the room is free from external noise.
- If a student is confused by a sentence, rephrase it, and

don't keep repeating the same sentence that they misunderstand.

Physical disabilities

- Find out what assistive technology is available.
- Arrange furniture to ensure the disabled person is in the group rather than sitting aside, and that there is safe circulation and access to materials and equipment for everyone.

Visual impairment

- Use assistive technology, e.g. JAWS software.
- Provide large-print handouts if appropriate, or a CSW.

Dyslexia

- Produce handouts on mauve or cream paper or other colours to suit the learner.
- Use a sans serif font such as **Comic Sans**.
- Change foreground and background colours on the computer to suit the learner.
- Discuss ways around difficulties with the learner, including Additional Learning Support.

Mental ill-health

- Discuss the issue with the student and explore ways to provide support.
- Be encouraging and supportive.
- Be flexible to allow the learner to feel comfortable and adjust to the new learning environment.
- If the student informs you, or you become aware of, occasional challenging behaviour, you should carry out a risk assessment, especially for vocational workshops with potentially hazardous equipment or materials.

People with dexterity difficulties

- Use computers with large or ergonomic keyboards.
- Make use of a note-taker. This could be a Dictaphone, so the learner can have the material translated into notes.

Speech and language difficulties

- Identify whether the problem is physical or cognitive.
- Give the learner time to respond and do not finish off the sentence for him or her.
- Be aware of strategies to allow a learner to join a discussion group.

As with all teaching, we need to work with individuals as part of a group. While we should not exclude anyone because of their disability, we also need to remember not to deny an activity to the whole class because of a learner's disability, as this could cause embarrassment to the learner.

The key to a positive experience for everyone is to have really good communications within the class, with other colleagues (such as the examinations officer or learning support tutor), with external partners including work experience employers and, where appropriate, with external agencies such as Equal People, social services or charities. As we are working with adult students, we should always be sensitive to confidentiality and individual dignity and check with the student before talking to other people about him or her.

Dealing with the subject of disability with our students

Language is dynamic and what is acceptable or 'politically correct' changes over time. There is a wide variation of usage, even among people with disabilities. Disabled people and their organizations try to define disability in terms of the Social Model of Disability,[11] and language is crucially important here. The social model identifies society's physical, sensory, attitudinal, legal and behavioural barriers as the factors that make people disabled, not particular medical conditions or impairments. Society also uses language that would not generally be used by members of the Disabled People's Movement.

If dealing with the subject of disability in class, we need to draw students' attention to the issues or barriers that affect the quality of life of disabled people, such as accessible transport, accessible housing, affordable healthcare, employment opportunities and discrimination, rather than focus on impairments or conditions (unless this is crucial to the document or discussion). Although it is sometimes difficult if we are using media stories as our source, we should try to avoid emotional stories about incurable diseases, congenital impairments or severe injuries. While stories about super-achievers (such as athletes with physical disabilities conquering Everest) sell papers, people with disabilities think that portraying disabled people in this way raises a false expectation that all disabled people should achieve this level, and would prefer us not to portray successful disabled people as superhuman. Similarly we need to be careful not to sensationalize disability by using phrases like 'afflicted with', 'suffers from', 'victim of', 'crippled with' and so on. We need instead to use and encourage our students to use phrases such as 'a person who has arthritis' or 'a woman who has cystic fibrosis'. In a sector in which social groups are routinely referred to by generic labels such as 'the deaf', 'the blind' or 'the disabled', we need to try to emphasize the person, not the impairment, and use phrases like 'person who is deaf', 'person who is blind' instead. Similarly, we need to focus on the individual and not on their particular impairment or condition. So 'children who are blind' is preferable to 'blind children'. There are obvious phrases that are totally unacceptable these days, but some disabled people also find euphemisms such as 'physically incapacitated' and 'visually challenged' to be condescending.

Age

Age is relative: if you are the only 30-year-old in a class of 16 to 19-year-olds you will be perceived and perceive yourself as 'older'. We need to ensure that we have strategies to manage differential age and experience so that all age groups benefit, and this does not just mean mixing 16 to 19-year-olds with adults. We shouldn't forget that the age gap between 30 and 60 is a lot greater than the gap between 18 and 30, and yet everyone over 19 tends to be seen as a homogeneous group.

There are some life transitions that are age-specific, such as the end of initial schooling, becoming a mother, menopause or retirement. We need to recognize this and cater for the emotional and educational needs of people of different ages within a mixed-age class. It is sometimes helpful to provide age-focused courses for groups such as young adults who are trying to overcome their experiences of social exclusion.

Young adults

The transition from childhood to adulthood is a challenging and complex process. Some young adults aged 19 to 24 experience considerable difficulties adjusting to new roles and responsibilities and find themselves excluded from mainstream society. Alcohol and drug abuse or a criminal record may contribute to their problems. For many, being a youth is not the only factor they have to manage: racial prejudice, low self-esteem linked to previous failure at school, poverty and the lack of social facilities all combine to socially exclude. (See Chapter 4 for successful curriculum initiatives.)

Older learners

Age – legislation and government education policy

In March 2005 the government launched its older people strategy Opportunity Age: Meeting the Challenges of Ageing in the 21st Century. The report spoke of the need to develop educational opportunities for older people. The strategy refers to the need for education and training for employability as well as the need to safeguard education for 'leisure, personal interest and community development purposes'.

From 2006, equal rights legislation makes age discrimination unlawful.

Age-related equal rights legislation will be in force from 2006. As people are living longer, governments are faced with managing the pension and health needs of a growing percentage of the population. Responses include investigating the economic contribution that older people can continue to make, and the role of education in maintaining physical and emotional health. This has implications for employers in terms of recruitment and training/re-training of older people, and for the National Health Service and social services. This is turn has implications for the learning and skills sector.

Dench and Regan (2000) found that 80% of learners aged 50 to 71 reported a positive impact of learning on at least one of the following areas: self confidence and self esteem; satisfaction with other aspects of their life; and their ability to cope. There is also evidence that the health-related benefits of learning include a reduction in reliance on medication and dependency on support services. This is an economic factor that governments should not ignore when funding adult learning.

According to NIACE analysis of the National Adult Learning Survey (NALS), over the past ten years participation figures have remained fairly static for people over 55. However, the statistics show that participation in learning activities declines with age and falls dramatically for those aged 65 and over:

Age group	Participation in learning activities currently or in past 3 years
20–24	63%
25–34	52%
35–44	49%
45–54	47%
55–64	32%
65–74	17%
75 and older	10%

Source: NIACE Briefing Sheet 69, Older People and Learning – Key Statistics, 2005.

More older learners participate in non-vocational, non-accredited courses than in vocational and accredited courses, with a significant number accessing learning provided by informal organizations. In FE colleges in 2004/5, the number of students aged over 56 enrolled on courses was 523,192 (61.3

per cent women, 38.7 per cent men) out of a total enrolment of 2.4 million adults.[12]

Despite the introduction of age discrimination legislation, I have some concerns about how well we prepare our mature students for re-entering the workplace. How do they fare as newly qualified entrants into professions such as teaching, social work and health at an age when those who have already had a career may be considering early retirement? Even if the post-school sector is not ageist, the world of work often is, particularly towards women. As Weiner and Maguire (1995) have argued, no age is the right age for a woman. She is either 'lacking experience and authority' or no longer 'young and bright'. Returning to education and gaining new skills and a new career can be hugely empowering, and I am sure that this is the experience of the majority of our students. We need to work closely with employers and higher education institutions to minimize the negative aspects that mature students may encounter.

Managing the ignorance or intolerance of others and improving practice

Our different histories and life experiences inform our attitudes. Many students and colleagues will use inappropriate language or behaviour out of ignorance rather than prejudice. We can all think of examples of our own unwitting actions that make us cringe. Most people are prepared to modify their behaviour when somebody has explained why that behaviour is intimidating or offensive to others. Inappropriate behaviour needs to be challenged rather than colluded with, and we need to have a variety of strategies to question assumptions, provide information and raise awareness if individuals are acting in a prejudiced way.

Direct discrimination needs immediate and tough action. Your organization's equality and diversity policy will state the procedures and sanctions for breach of legal and college regulations and standards. Ensure that you are clear about your responsibilities and that you know where you can get support.

We have a professional duty to ensure that all members of the learning community in our organization feel respected and valued. If we notice anything that the organization could do to improve the experience of staff or students, or help attract a wider, more diverse group of people to courses, we should raise this with the relevant manager or committee.

The majority of people working in the learning and skills sector have a massive personal commitment to equality and social justice. While the imposition of policies and monitoring is intended to improve the experience for learners, the real drive for change comes from within. We should never forget the contribution that each of us can make to the culture of our organization and the success of individuals.

See Appendix II for a list of national organizations that provide information and services and can also advise you on local agencies to support work on equality and diversity.

Notes

[1] Also seen in the 'Welfare to Work' changes in the state benefits system.

[2] The committee remit was to recommend how strategies, including the funding methodology, could be developed to increase and improve the quality of participation; how good practice could be shared; and how the effect of its strategies might be monitored and evaluated (FEFC 1997).

[3] This initiative focused on developing policies and strategies to ensure that no social group is excluded from education. The emphasis is on responding to individual student needs within a group, e.g. differentiation, personal tutorial (FEFC 1998). Information is available on the LSC website.

[4] This is detailed in *The Common Inspection Framework 2005* (Ofsted, website only). Monitoring includes: observation of teaching; analysis of student participation and success rates broken down by race, gender and disability; and meetings with students.

[5] I am using the concept of discourse as related to the work of Michel Foucault (1977). This position suggests that notions of common sense and rationality are expressed by the dominant culture through culturally specific ideas set in public policy. These dominant discourses have the power to 'silence' or marginalize alternative discourses. However, it is possible for individuals to deconstruct these powerful discourses by revealing contradictions, diversity and alternative

perspectives, and this has the potential to subvert discourses, which then offers the potential of empowerment to oppressed groups.

6   Robertson has argued that many educational institutions find it difficult to accept research that indicates that they are involved in systematic bias. In relation to gender bias, she suggests that the dominant male discourse cloaks itself in the 'mannerisms of impartiality' (Robertson 1992: 58).

7   Centre for Excellence in Leadership research, *Leading Change in Equality and Diversity*, 2005.

8   Further reading on why some people remain disaffected can be found in a number of NIACE publications that draw on surveys and empirical research.

9   'Habitus' has been developed as a concept by Bourdieu (Bourdieu and Passeron 1990; Bourdieu and Wacquant 1992) to demonstrate how an individual is placed within the social world and also to demonstrate the way in which the key aspects of culture are embodied within an individual, evident in the way in which he or she is disposed to think, feel and behave. Bourdieu's theorization shifts class from a simple categorization based on economic or social status to a complex web of relationships between and within classes. 'Habitus' provides a conceptual tool for recognizing differences between individuals within the same cultural group, and emphasizes the inequalities that permeate those differences.

10 A number of studies have been concerned with the experiences of mature women students, notably Morrison (1992) and Edwards (1993). Although these studies are predominantly about women students in higher education, the findings correlate with my own research on the experience of women in FE (Hayes 1999).

11 Further information can be obtained from www.skill.org.uk

12 Source: LSC statistics department.

4 Effective strategies to widen participation

Market research and publicity

In the years of growth following incorporation in 1993, colleges greatly expanded their provision for adults in order to meet their growth targets and benefit from increased funding. Most colleges began to invest heavily in market research and publicity, sometimes at the expense of more direct and 'personal' recruitment methods such as community outreach workers. The increase in expenditure in FE in high-quality colour brochures, media advertisements and a more professional 'front of house' style, reminiscent perhaps of a high street building society, has been described by Gerwirtz et al. (1995) as 'glossification'.

Marketing and services to business units within colleges work with brokers and their local LSC research department to identify and meet local employment and training needs. FE has had to develop a range of styles to engage a broad range of client groups; the presentation and approach required to respond to the expectations of a large multi-national employer is not the same as that which will inspire the confidence and trust of local unemployed people. Our problem is not merely attracting students: we have to recruit people who are prepared to pay fees and other course costs, or who attract government funding. Colleges therefore have the dual and sometimes conflicting role of responding to student demand and providing what the LSC will pay for.[1]

Despite an increase in the public funding of education, recent government priorities have been focused on the 14 to 19-year-old cohort. Since 2005, funding for adult learners has reduced. Obviously not all demands can be met and therefore funding of adult education and training are being targeted at people with low basic skills and qualification levels. The pressure on providers is to achieve enough applications to be able to meet their LSC recruitment and funding targets and maintain or improve their student success rates.

Examination of UK demography shows that the diminishing cohorts of young people can only fill one in three of the vacancies for new and replacement jobs expected over the next decade. The other places will need to be filled by people currently outside the labour force and by older people taking on new roles. Yet on the evidence of recent NIACE surveys (Aldridge and Tunkett 2004, 2005), these groups remain the least likely to participate in adult learning.[2]

The more colleges market themselves with glossy publications and the attributes of business, the less easy it becomes for students with low confidence to seek access. Crossing the college threshold is a major step for many who have not been successful in their initial education. Imposing entrances, uniformed staff and security systems are additional obstacles to people who lack confidence and feel that *Education's for Other People* (McGivney 1990). While telephone and on-line enrolment, and payment by credit card suit the lifestyle of those who have already achieved, it is another barrier for people living in temporary accommodation, who have limited language and literacy, and who rely on cash. We therefore need to find other ways to engage people from these groups. The ALI Chief Inspector's report identifies 'sound technical practice in recruiting, initially assessing and inducting learners' as underpinning the practice of top quality providers (see www.ali.gov.uk).

What adults want from course information

This is not the same as what educators think they want or provide!

Prospectus and leaflets with full and accurate information on programmes including entry requirements, course content, college services, academic and social facilities. An estimate of real costs and time commitment outside college.

Information about the other students (especially age profile). Progression pathways to and from courses and the actual destinations of previous students: short case studies with photographs are always good. The cost and average time of travelling between sites by public transport and any help with travel such as lift schemes.

Website that is easy to navigate with more information than a prospectus, e.g. video clips of performances and exhibitions. See for example the City Literary Institute (www.citylit.ac.uk), the Mary Ward Centre (www.marywardcentre.ac.uk) and Kensington and Chelsea College (www.kcc.ac.uk).

Course/programme handbooks that include full and accurate information on the syllabus, teaching and learning methods, qualifications and progression routes. Details and a timetable of assignments help students to be clear about what is required, when it is required and the criteria to be used for assessment. Lists of key staff and services and how to access them are also useful.

Taster sessions, which allow potential students to visit the college/organization to see the facilities, meet the lecturer and perhaps current students and ask questions. Models include having the first session as a taster, open days and 'bring a friend' sessions. These work well as group visits planned in partnership with community organizations (transport provided) or to encourage lower-level students taught in community venues to progress into higher-level college courses.

Pre-course advice and guidance. Models include: presentation/ group interview sessions organized by curriculum staff who teach the programme; general advice sessions with guidance staff and some specialists (regular times or drop-in); individual interviews/action planning, which may include diagnostic testing.

Introductory/diagnostic courses. The idea of interviews and 'testing' can be a barrier to some students. Open access courses, which are designed to build student confidence and identify skills and learning needs, allow students a little more time to adjust to returning to learning and make informed choices about suitable programmes. These are especially helpful when students are looking to education to help them make a life change but may not yet be sure of the precise vocational direction they would like this change to take.

Information should be provided in a way that is accessible to people with disabilities, and in community languages, as appropriate.

Widening participation and learning pathways projects

Following the Kennedy Report (FEFC 1997), 'widening participation' was made a priority for the post-compulsory sector. The government funded a number of projects through the Adult and Community Learning Fund[3] and other widening participation projects in order to attract new students back into education through imaginative community initiatives that might reach people not attracted by the standard marketing and publicity. Some of the best examples can be found in Greenwood et al. 2000 and Champney et al. 2005.[4] A recent research project (Taylor et al. 2004)[5] undertaken by the Institute of Education in London set out to identify strategies that have been reliably proven to raise participation in learning by adults from social groups with traditionally low participation. They concluded that because of the lack of effective evaluation in the field, none of the strategies investigated could be reliably proved or disproved to raise participation rates. The most promising strategies were found to be learner-centred and congruent with those advocated in the LSC (2003) document *Successful Participation for All*. Unsurprisingly they found that recruitment and retention of students from non-participant groups is complex, and because of the unpredictable interaction of many different factors there is no magical formula. However, the box below identifies key elements that are thought to contribute to success. They certainly match my own experience.

Effective strategies to widen participation

Outreach, targeting and engagement

- Activities in the community, especially personal 'word of mouth' recommendation, can attract new learners from minority groups.
- Collaborative projects between organizations that are able to provide flexible support and provision tailored to the specific needs of individuals are more likely to engage 'hard-to-reach learners'.
- A sound understanding by providers of the pressures and motivators for learners can lead to pre-emptive action to reduce disengagement.
- Support from external agencies, such as NIACE and trade unions, can bring about partnership working between community organizations and employers which engages new learners.

Participation and retention

- Good communication between learners, educators and employers about motivation and barriers to accessing education results in the design of relevant programmes and good retention.
- Teaching methods, learning and learner support need to be sensitive to the needs of the individuals and applied from the earliest stages.
- Flexible funding to support the development and delivery of innovative provision has resulted in effective work with hard-to-reach groups.

Achievement and progression

- There needs to be a good 'fit' between learner expectations of themselves and the objectives of the course.
- Appropriate assessment of learner progress needs to be in place to motivate learners and support progression to further study or employment.
- High levels of learner support are required for 'hard-to-reach' groups and students with learning difficulties.

- Success requires skilled and experienced staff with good contacts in other local agencies to support the development of learning pathways and help individuals progress.
- Workforce development programmes with basic skills embedded have a positive impact on learner self-esteem, quality of work and economic position.

See Champney *et al.* (2005) and the NIACE website for case studies of successful projects.

The implications of this report are that we need to work with community organizations and employers to develop more flexibility of provision in order to meet the needs of the workplace. However, as already discussed, this is not without its problems: first, the difficulties of successfully engaging employers to raise the skills of employees and potential employees; second, the short-term nature of project funding that is available to pilot new initiatives; and finally, the values and cultures of education and business can run counter to the maintenance of personal identity. There remains considerable anger and hostility, among the most 'hard-to-reach' groups of adults, towards an education system which was seen to be trying to impose and uphold the values of a particular class and culture. Non-participation may not therefore imply antipathy towards education so much as to the nature of the education on offer (McGivney 1990, 1996). Some successful projects are described in the box below.

Attracting and retaining disengaged young adults[6]

Successful projects

Northallerton Wheels in North Yorkshire used skate-boarding as a way of introducing a group of young men to using ICT and multimedia skills. The motivation was the creation of a website and promotional information as part of their campaign to obtain a local skate park.

Musicscool was able to attract 'bedroom musicians' because it gave them access to state-of-the-art music equipment and IT software.

Second Wave in South East London used volunteers as role models to work as 'trusted intermediaries' with a group of black young men in a performance arts project. It encouraged these learners to examine their experience of the inner city including self-protection, racism, empowerment and survival in a creative and challenging way through hip-hop and rap, street dance, vocals and song writing. Exploring these themes in this way developed interpersonal and professional skills.

Key characteristics

- Activities are real for the learner and build on their existing interests and enthusiasms, such as rap music, DJing or street fashion.
- As students progress, they are encouraged to take on volunteering roles, which brings a constant flow of new adults with fresh ideas into the organization and provides positive role models.
- The approach is respectful of and celebrates the cultural context of students. This may include ensuring that staff reflect the characteristics of the target group through age, sexual orientation, gender, ethnicity and disability.
- A sense of ownership of the learning context and process is created by involving students in planning, management and development of a project. Activities might include creating a student management group that allocates roles and responsibilities and evaluates progress. Planning, negotiation within the team and with external agencies, analysis and evaluation can take place in a safe environment supporting the development of wider key skills, confidence and self esteem.[7]
- An alternative attendance mode, teaching and learning approach to school is offered. This might include: whole group work, one-to-one support and mentoring, a residential element to 'bond' the group early on, and occasional outings and social events linked to the course.
- Activities take place, if possible, in a venue that is not

reminiscent of 'school'. This is where performing arts and community projects can excel.

• Positive relationships between staff and learners are developed. The ability to develop an atmosphere of trust and mutual respect is crucial.

• New technology is used. The opportunity to learn about and use new technology is an important incentive for young people (men in particular) to engage in learning.

• Holistic support is provided. Successful projects ensure that students can focus on learning because other life pressures such as ill health or housing are supported through effective multi-agency communication.[8] Also find out about local agencies including Connexions, the probation service, arts partnerships, social services, primary care trusts and charities.

• The approach encourages students to explore their own emotions and feelings and address personal issues that they may find it difficult to talk about through the learning process. Performance-based subjects are excellent for this. Drama techniques can be used within other subject areas to examine experiences and social issues, but knowing the boundaries and where to refer students is important in order to manage feelings about the issues raised.

Pre-course information, advice and guidance

Becoming a student is exciting but it may also be daunting: it is both full of possibilities and full of practical problems and academic and emotional challenges. For many people, the biggest challenge of all is to cross the threshold of an educational institution. 'Cleo' told me that she had received pre-course advice and guidance on several occasions, over a period of two or three years, before she finally enrolled on an Access course:

I'd get as far as going to the careers officer and then I'd go back to square one just working and working and earning a wage ... I think that for anyone going back to education, you know, it may be your dream and you say 'Oh yes', but it may be quite a long process. It's not going to be easy, you know, you can't just jump into a diploma or a degree, obviously, and you have to start from the bottom, which is a bit off-putting. I don't think anybody means to put you off, but it depends on how you feel at the time.

The quality of pre-entry information, advice and guidance influences participation and affects students' choice of courses and their subsequent achievements. We need to achieve a balance between marketing courses to attract target numbers and giving potential students impartial guidance on appropriate course choice. At course level, there is a tension between selection that may be experienced as threatening and erode fragile confidence, and ensuring that students have a clear and realistic idea of what will be expected of them in order to complete the course successfully. We must not let the pressure to interview students and meet recruitment targets result in inadequate discussion with them about the demands that becoming a student will make, not only in college, but also on their home lives, as this can build problems for the future. A college counsellor who supports students experiencing stress told me:

I've been finding people taking rather an instant decision to come on to the course, if there was a place available, without having actually thought through the implications for them.

Our failure to discuss students' aspirations and course requirements fully may allow them to have false expectations of the course, or themselves, which could lead to early withdrawal, or poor achievement with consequent loss of revenue for the college, quite apart from the loss of self-esteem or confidence in the education system that the student may experience.

Reisenberger and Sadler (1997) have discussed the growth of centralized guidance and admissions units with dedicated staff in FE colleges, and Martinez (1997) presents some different admissions models employed in the FE sector. Payne and

Edwards' (1997) research into in-house college guidance has revealed a complex picture in which impartiality is only one aspect of guidance and there is the possibility, in practice, of different interpretations of an institution's professional codes and quality frameworks. While the shift has been towards qualified guidance staff providing pre- and on-course information and advice about progression to work or further study, lecturers will always have a crucial role. One reason for this is that the majority of adult students are part-time and the person they know and have easy access to is their lecturer. Also, their lecturer is qualified in the subject area they are studying and may well be a practising professional with current contacts in their vocational or academic field. The pivotal role of the lecturer or 'tutor' can not be over-emphazised, and students often want to meet and 'check out' the person who is going to teach them (especially if they have had unfortunate experiences of teachers in the past). This of course is not always possible.

Student choices and equal opportunities

How can we as education professionals ensure that all students have equal opportunities to make 'real choices'? This is a challenge. The reduction in the number of easy access 'leisure' and non-accredited courses, which many have used as a first step back into education, along with an increase in fees means that people with few qualifications and low incomes are likely to have their choice limited to a basic skills or vocational course at or below level 2. We need to find ways of making sure that students make informed choices about courses and are not limited by material circumstances and social expectations.

In Chapter 1 we considered some of the social and economic factors that motivate adults to return to education. Some students have a clear aim, which may be work-related, or a personal interest. There are others who are hoping not just to gain a qualification but to improve their status and lifestyle:

I'd like to secure a better future for me and my son and also set a good example for him as well. Having a kid makes you evaluate your life a bit more. You know, you want more out of it. It's not just the money, I'd like him to be proud of me, especially as I'm his main role model.

Although motivated to return to education in order to change aspects of their lives, the initial choices of courses and future careers that students make are often still based on traditional gendered skills. For example, women often migrate towards courses such as childcare, nursing, hairdressing and beauty therapy. Choice may also be made according to cultural dispositions and familial 'habituses'. Some career paths may not be considered because there is a belief that certain areas of study are part of the culture pattern of higher socio-economic groups and therefore are for 'others'.

We have a professional duty to challenge the social structures that limit horizons and to make sure that students do not set targets below their abilities, or fail to 'follow their dreams'. Yet at the same time we need to be aware of the pressure that being ambitious and challenging stereotypes can bring on individuals, as is illustrated by one of my college students:

> My dad thinks I'm a dosser and going to college is an excuse for not going to work because he thinks women shouldn't have ambitions, you know, any old job that comes along albeit cleaning or shops, as long as you're bringing in money and not poncing off the tax payer, or him.[9]

Students therefore make their choices in a complex multi-layered context in which college, friendships, family, the media and wider social attitudes all impact (Reay 1998).

Selection

Once a student has decided to apply for entry to college, we have the job of selection. For some basic level short courses there may be open entry, but for substantial part-time and full-time courses there will be entry requirements and some form of selection test. While younger students' qualifications are a fair predictor of skills because they are recent, this is not the same for adults. Skills need to be maintained: an old GCE 'O' level in home economics is not going to be much help for someone applying to do a professional catering course, yet recent catering experience, even without a qualification, may be.

The search for more effective recruitment procedures has driven some of the research into student retention, with managers looking for indicators of the characteristics of the 'successful student'. Martinez (1997) suggests that reliable and robust procedures can be established to identify students at risk of dropping out. However, McGivney's (1996) research discusses the problems involved in trying to discern trends in current retention and achievement data. She argues that past performance is not a good prediction of future outcomes and warns against attempts to devise a typology of students likely to be vulnerable to early withdrawal. My own research findings (Hayes 1999) similarly demonstrate that a poor academic record in initial education, and perhaps non-completion of courses in adulthood, does not necessarily mean that an individual will not be successful in terms of both institutional outcomes and personal learning goals; he or she may, however, need extra time and support.

It is beyond the scope of this book to discuss interviewing and selection in detail: your department, college or other institution will have systems in place. These should ensure access to students with disabilities, which may mean special arrangements for interviewing, such as hearing loop provision or signers. The best advice is to treat adult students as we would wish to be treated ourselves and never make assumptions about them, or what they are capable of achieving.

Pre-entry screening, placement and diagnostic tests

These phrases sound horrible and are definitely not what most students want to hear. However, students probably expect some sort of selection interview and to bring a portfolio of work if they are applying for an art course, or to audition for a performing arts course. Most FE colleges now use screening or diagnostic tests in order to place students on appropriate courses or identify support needs.[10] Despite the increase in the volume of initial assessment now taking place, the ALI[11] has judged it to be poor across the sector so it is something we need to think about.

The national 'placement' tests for language, literacy and numeracy (LLN) are becoming an integral part of selection for most FE courses. The tests are short and easy to administer. They are completely objective and can be marked by any lecturer. The score relates to a level[12] and from there it is easy to decide whether the student is able to cope with the reading, writing or number element of their vocational course. Decisions on whether support should be embedded, 'bolt on' or Additional Learning Support (ALS) are taken from there. Practitioners have found that the English for Speakers of Other Languages (ESOL) test is too unwieldy for a non-specialist, but some colleges have developed their own versions, accompanied by very clear guidelines that vocational staff can use as a starting point. If we can create a relaxed atmosphere, present the tests as a completely normal part of induction and explain the advantages to students, even unconfident ones will take these in their stride.

Do not confuse placement tests for LLN with diagnostic testing for LLN. The diagnostic tests are altogether different. They need to be administered and marked by a specialist and are part of ESOL or basic skills courses or ALS.

Testing, screening and otherwise selecting students according to their previous academic achievement, current competencies, personality profile or personal circumstance is only the first part of their experience of returning to education. However thorough the pre-entry system, it is unlikely to prepare students for the challenge of becoming a mature student. There will also be people who have needs that are not picked up or whose circumstances change, perhaps through illness. We need to watch for signs of students having difficulties and be ready to take appropriate action, such as transferring them to a different course or referring them for additional support. In Chapter 7 we will look at the support needs of adult students from induction through to progression and careers advice.

Notes

1   In 2005 LSCs defined courses that were not on the National Qualification Framework as 'other provision' and put the funding of these courses at risk. The designation included courses, such as first aid, which were required by industry, and other courses that had been designed to encourage and widen participation, many validated by the OCN.

2   The NALS Survey (NIACE) researches adult participation in learning in the UK. Using the responses of around 5,000 adults, it offers key findings, and breaks down participation, trends in participation and future intentions to learn by gender, socio-economic class, age, employment and the regions.

3   The Adult and Community Learning Fund was launched by the government in 1998 as part of its strategy to widen participation in learning and improve standards of basic skills. The fund makes the important connection between learning and social regeneration.

4   This excellent toolkit presents a set of case studies from colleges and community organizations, with practical suggestions and techniques for widening participation (book and CD-ROM).

5   The research focused on 82 relevant studies undertaken from 1992 onwards.

6   Example from NIACE/NYA report identifying best practice in Adult and Community Learning Fund projects.

7   Skills for Life (literacy, numeracy and language) and the wider key skills can be embedded within such vocational courses or community projects www.niace.org.uk/Research/YALP/Documents/ACLF-final-report.pdf.

8   See Appendix 2 for a list of national organisations to act as a starting point for you to make your own links.

9   'Michelle' left school at 16 with no qualifications. She returned to college at 21 and studied GCSE English and mathematics before taking an Access course. She eventually progressed to a degree course in journalism.

10   The Skills for Life tests have been devised and tested to remove cultural bias. If you are devising your own vocational tasks, take care not to exclude some social groups through your use of language or cultural bias.

11   Source: Richard Moore, ALI inspector, reporting key findings at the Central London Learning Partnership Conference, May 2005.

12   Vocational lecturers should have training, however, as the interpretation of entry 1, 2, 3 and levels 1 and 2 do not quite match the vocational counterpart.

5 Getting down to teaching and learning

Learning in FE

Learning is a complex cultural activity and success relies on getting the inter-relationship between a number of factors right. The students themselves, through their backgrounds, disposition and attitudes to learning and FE, have a major influence. The experience that we bring to teaching adults includes subject expertise and teaching skill, but also our own values and perhaps prejudices. There are opportunities and constraints offered by accommodation and equipment. The syllabus, with its particular content and assessment requirements, is a key aspect. Government and local policies and priorities, inspection, performance measures, employment opportunities, vocational and academic cultures all play their part in influencing the learning environment.

Hopefully, our students learn the things we teach them, but they also learn other things. Much informal learning results in greater student confidence and self-esteem, but some is damaging, such as discovering that they do not have an aptitude for the subject of their choice, or that they do not fit into the dominant college or workplace cultures – although if we spot signs of this early on, we may be able to take remedial action.

In earlier chapters, I have detailed the context within which adults learn and some successful strategies that you can apply to your own teaching. This chapter focuses on some basics of adult teaching and learning. If you have little experience of teaching adults, it gives you some tried-and-tested starting points. If you are more experienced, it should help you to reflect on your practice.

Getting started

I have emphasized that every piece of paper or personal contact that the student has had prior to arriving in our classroom should give them clear and accurate information about the course. However, we still need to check what students' expectations are of the course and the organization, especially if they enrolled directly, or were interviewed by someone else. By making introductions and describing the course content and outcomes, we give people the opportunity to settle down before they have to do anything. This is also a way of establishing that everyone is in the right room – it is not unknown at the start of the year, with room changes and temporary staff on reception, for students or even staff to be in the wrong place!

We need to identify at the outset: the likely cost of materials and equipment students will have to buy; the amount of time they will need to plan for study outside class times; dates and costs of additional activities such as theatre, museum or field trips; and the dates of assessments or examinations if they are on different days from the course. Remember that features we have planned to enhance studies and help the group to 'gel' may cause problems, for example for someone on a low income who has to pay for a babysitter as well as for the event itself, so give plenty of notice of the dates of special events, which are probably not detailed in the pre-course literature. We should also give students information about any financial assistance available for on-course costs.

Things to cover in the first class

- Basic administration, such as registration.
- Course aims and objectives – what your students will have learnt/be able to do by the end of the course (see next box).
- How far the content can be negotiated around students' needs and interests.
- Equipment, books and materials, their likely cost and good places to get them.

- Health and safety (special forms may be required for some activities).
- Local information such as library, refectory, bookshop and crèche or nursery opening times.
- Resources and services to support learning.
- Study circles or 'buddies' if you have them.[1]
- Activities that help students get to know each other.
- What to bring/do for next week.
- Friendly informal introduction to all students: their names and something about their backgrounds and interests.
- Contacts for you/the institution in case of enquiries or absence.

Back this up with a course information sheet or handbook. Students' abilities to absorb large amounts of complex information about the course will be limited in the first session, as their main anxiety will probably be about 'fitting in' with the group.

Don't get confused by aims and objectives

Aims are general statements of intent about the purpose of the whole programme. They should be limited to just a few. They are usually long-term goals.

Objectives are specific and detail the learning steps students will take to achieve the course aims. Each class should have clear objectives that you share with your students at the start and then re-visit at the end to see if they have been achieved. A helpful way of defining objectives is to say, 'by the end of the class students will be able to . . .'. Use action words that you can measure such as 'identify', 'select', 'demonstrate'. Beware of words like 'understand'. You need measurements that prove that learning has taken place.

Style is as important as content

It is a favourite quip amongst adult educators that the first thing you do is to re-arrange the furniture, but in fact getting the ambience right is very important. Arranging chairs and tables in a U shape or circle means that everyone can have eye contact with each other and feel included. Obviously, workshops and studios require their own layout. If you know that you have a student with a disability, ensure that your layout includes them – no wheelchairs at the back or outside the circle.

We need to think carefully about how to cover any administrative aspect without detracting from the 'main event'. Timing is crucial. It is helpful to cover matters such as emergency exits and the register early on, but get into the 'meat' of the session as soon as possible – that is what they have come for.

By our own demeanour and the type of activities we employ, we can help students feel at ease with each other and with us. Beware of 'ice-breakers', which were fashionable several years ago. They can be effective in certain situations, but if you employ an over-elaborate one, your students may feel awkward or think you are doing a David Brent[2] impression. Think of activities that can actively involve everyone without anyone feeling over-exposed. Getting students to work in pairs or small groups can be effective: for example, ask them to talk to the person next to them, to find out their name and one thing they hope to gain from the course and then tell the rest of the group about this person. People are often more willing to introduce another person to the group than themselves and we can begin to get a feel for personalities and what we need to do to create a purposeful group atmosphere in which everyone is valued.

Get people actively involved as soon as possible. Talking 'at' them for a whole class is a turn-off, although they will probably be too polite to let you know. A well-chosen task is diagnostic and can help us begin to identify aptitudes and skills gaps, perhaps building on pre-entry information we already have. Try to do something that will cater for the different life experiences, learning needs and personalities in the group.

Underpinning all this is the need to inspire and motivate adult learners from the very start. One way of doing this is to think about situations that have inspired you. Those that have had the opposite effect are also useful to reflect on!

Lecturer's survival checklist for the first session

- Prepare samples, slides and handouts the day before – no last-minute photocopying.
- Arrive in the classroom in good time and check the technology is working and furniture arrangement is suitable.
- Remove traces of the previous class, e.g. clean the whiteboard and have a fresh piece of paper on the flipchart.
- Do something interesting to set the mood, e.g. play music from the period in an art history or literature course, or from the relevant foreign country in a language or food studies class. Smell and taste are very evocative – you may be able to think of some interesting uses in your class.
- Introduce yourself to each student as they arrive – a brief chat will give you some indications of their previous experience and expectations.
- Start promptly – as you mean to go on, five minutes' delay maximum. You may want to state the policy on punctuality and regular attendance, or draw up a class contract.[3]
- Cover 'domestic arrangements' such as emergency procedures and the policy on mobile telephones. A student who is self-employed or a parent/carer may wish or need to be in instant contact with the outside world, but it can be disruptive of the session.
- Share the objectives for the session at the start.
- In addition to specialist materials and equipment, have a juicy pen for overhead projector, flipchart or whiteboard but never ever use them on an interactive whiteboard.
- Take extra pens, paper or other appropriate bits and pieces for the students who did not know what to bring in the first week.

- Keep student work or take a photograph of it in the first session of a practical course. You can then look at it later with the class to show what progress has been made. This is also useful evidence for inspectors. (Video is also useful to record progress – but probably a little threatening in the first class.)
- Evaluate the session. What evidence do you have that learning took place? Note what went well and changes to make for next time.

By the end of the first class, every student should have had the opportunity to make a contribution and they should all leave with something made or learnt. It is important that we summarize what has been covered in the class and identify how well the learning that has taken place meets the session objectives. Give students a tantalizing glimpse of what they are going to do the next week and be clear about anything they have to do in advance or bring to the next class. Always leave them wanting more.

Whereas younger students cannot wait to get out of the door, this is the moment when some adult students will want to ask you questions that they may not have felt comfortable about raising in class. Make time for this, as you can gain valuable insights into the motivations and anxieties of your students, which you can use to make your sessions positive for them. Say a personal goodbye to each person, but beware of getting over-involved in personal matters.

Content and materials

The teaching materials we use need to be appropriate and engaging for adults. Your department will probably have a resource bank, but it may be rather 16–18 orientated, or just plain dated. For example, in foreign language teaching the quality of materials differs from language to language. Some, like Spanish, French and Italian, are richly resourced, with text books, Internet, CD-ROMs, cinema and modern visuals. Others are stuck in the Dark Ages. Academic and learning resource staff are always happy to signpost you to other resources, so ask! Whatever is available, it's always good to create your own really up-to-date resources using magazines, newspapers and the Internet.

Once we have got to know our students, we need to judge how much depth particular parts of the syllabus need to be covered in. Adult students will become bored if they spend a lot of time going over things they already know, but the chances are that your group will be 'mixed experience and mixed ability' so you will need to plan in some differentiation to enable people to work at their own speed.

Whenever possible, we should involve our students in decisions about the course, usually referred to as 'negotiating the curriculum'. We need to be clear about which aspects are negotiable and which are not and the consequences of any particular choice, in order to avoid any false expectations and discontent in the future.

By involving our students in discussion about the objectives, the way the course is planned and delivered and how it will be evaluated, we are recognizing their status as adults and treating them as equals. This involvement highlights their responsibility for their own learning, but we of course remain responsible for the quality of the course. While many students will find this motivating, there may be some who think – often because of their prior experience of education – that all the decisions are the lecturer's responsibility. We also need to beware of false consensus, with one or two powerful and confident voices dominating.

Teaching and learning

ALI's judgement of teaching and learning is that 60 per cent of lessons are good or better, but that too narrow a range of teaching methods is employed.[4] Even if our organization receives good inspection grades, we can always do better. Generally, what constitutes good teaching and learning can be applied across the LSC sector and is well identified in the Common Inspection Framework. However, if you are new to teaching adults the following points may be helpful.

- *Share session objectives* and ensure they are understood by learners and meet course requirements.

- *Keep up to date.* Feel confident to break away from education and subject traditions. Just because you were taught colour theory by spending hours painting the colour wheel does not make it the most effective or stimulating way to get the information across to your students.
- *Use a variety of teaching and learning methods,* but make sure you are confident. Don't experiment with PowerPoint or an interactive whiteboard if you've only had one lesson on it.
- *Encourage students to use new technologies* in class and for home study. Some will be familiar with them from their previous education or work; others may have gaps in their experience or knowledge. Never assume that all students have access to the Internet (or the personal skills and confidence to navigate it) in order to do their home assignments (unless yours is an ICT-based course in which this is already an established requirement).
- *Make adjustments for students with learning difficulties or disabilities.* This may mean arranging for special equipment such as a portable audio-loop for students with a hearing impairment (see page 41). Remember to ask students (discreetly) what would help them.
- *Ensure an appropriate variety and pace* by allowing sufficient time for a range of activities, including practising skills. Attention span affects memory, so we need to plan for different activities and changes of pace. Include a break, especially in evening classes, as people's ability to interact and retain information diminishes with fatigue. There are visual, auditory and kinaesthetic aspects to learning and the more variety in teaching techniques we use, the more effective the learning.
- *Manage mixed level/mixed ability* by dividing the class into sub-groups so that they can work at a pace and style that meets their needs. The 'plate-spinning' method, in which the lecturer rushes round servicing the needs of each individual in turn, is not recommended. It inevitably leaves some students sitting around waiting and bored. This is not the 'workshop method', which is what I have often been told! If students are working on a project, there

should be times when the whole group comes together. Use times when several students encounter a similar problem to draw together an *ad hoc* mini-group to share the learning point. This ensures efficient use of your time and encourages students to help each other.

- *Encourage student interaction.* When students work independently in practical subjects, it is possible for someone to spend a whole term talking only to the lecturer and not integrating with the group. Don't forget the social aspect of joining a course.

- *Use adult students' prior knowledge and experience as a resource.* If you draw theory from practice you engage students and make them feel valued. You may learn something yourself. One of the biggest problems I see when observing classes is too much teaching and not enough learning. Beware of trying to tell students everything you know about a particular topic, even if you have your Equity Card for entertainment skills.

- *Check that your students are learning.* Use question-and-answer and observation of practical work to check that they have understood and can apply their new knowledge.

- *Consider the practical implications for students of 'out of college' study.* Courses for adults are often condensed into a short time frame, e.g. one-year A-levels. Private study is a way of covering more ground, but this can pose real problems for some students who lack quiet space at home.

- *Identify learning support needs quickly* and make appropriate referrals. However, adults have had years to learn how to hide problems, so raise issues about skills gaps sensitively.

- *Make your classes stimulating, challenging and fun.*

- *Integrate theory along with practice and frequently check understanding.* To ensure effective learning, plan classes so that students can be involved in activities, reflect on their experience, gain a theoretical context and apply what they learn.[5]

- *Use tutorials* as a teaching method and integral to the way you work, not an 'add on'.

- *Assess progress and keep appropriate records.*

A sense of belonging to the class and the college

A significant factor affecting student retention is how integrated they feel (see Chapter 6). When students ask about the course prior to enrolment, their concerns are often as much about, 'Will there be people like me there?' as, 'Is the content what I want?' Our responsibility is to help the group to gel so that all members feel included and valued. Achieving this in a class in which some students already know each other and the college can be a challenge. It can be difficult for a new lecturer to take over an established class, let alone a new student to infiltrate some established groups. We need to create an atmosphere of trust in which people can air their views without fear of looking foolish, but where disrespect in terms of prejudice or self-centredness is effectively managed. If we can establish a supportive group, it allows people to experiment with new skills and ideas and to grow in confidence. The effect can reach beyond the class, so that students contact absent colleagues with class notes, give each other lifts and meet for a coffee when one of them is suffering a crisis of confidence.

Health and safety

Our employer is responsible for providing a healthy and safe work environment and training to ensure that employees are aware of their legal responsibilities. We are responsible for keeping up to date on legislation as it pertains to our specialism and for operating local systems such as carrying out risk assessments, and using substances according to Control of Substances Hazardous to Health (COSHH) regulations. Although the 'duty of care' for 16 to 19-year-olds is substantial, do not forget that most health and safety regulations still apply to adults. This includes educational visits and emergency evacuation. We need to be sure that all our students understand and comply with emergency evacuation for any class members with learning difficulties or disabilities. It is important, for example, that we ensure that students who are deaf understand what to do in situations in which they cannot hear the fire alarm, and that those with mobility problems are able to evacuate the building without a problem.

Final thoughts

Finally, recent research into learning in FE (Hodkinson and James 2003: 402) concluded, 'our data supports the view that teaching is an art rather than a technical craft' and,

> often the good pedagogy we observed did not fit the criteria set out for national standards and inspection criteria and what worked well for one tutor in one site, would not have worked for a different tutor or on a different site.' (Hodkinson 2005)

We therefore must continuously apply judgement and reflect on our practice. The most important thing we can do is listen to our students individually and as a group, and act on what they tell us. Through doing this, we discover that the potential for further improvement to learning is considerable because, 'Despite the significance of other factors, the dispositions and actions of a tutor have a major influence on learning' (Hodkinson and James 2003: 402).

Notes

[1] See Chapter 7 on student support and Chapter 6 on retention, which explain how these strategies may help some students.

[2] The embarrassingly awful boss in the British television series *The Office*.

[3] Strategies for managing punctuality and attendance are dealt with in Chapter 6.

[4] Based on the observation of 12,000 lessons as part of 135 inspections. Source: Richard Moore, ALI inspector, reporting key findings at the Central London Learning Partnership Conference, May 2005.

[5] Following Kolb's Experential Learning Cycle.

6 Improving punctuality and attendance

There is nothing more demoralizing than getting out of a warm bed on a dark, cold morning, struggling through the traffic to college, arriving fully prepared to deliver the most relevant and stimulating lesson of your life, only to sit in your teaching room waiting for your students (many of whom only live round the corner) to dribble in with an unimaginative array of excuses for lateness. Similarly, finding ways to ensure that students who miss classes don't fall behind or disrupt the learning of others places additional demands on us. We have to find a balance between being sympathetic to the very real problems that our adult students face and demanding commitment from them. This chapter will consider the pressures on adult students that lead to lack of punctuality and intermittent attendance, and which may result in them not completing their courses. Leaving a course before the end is very damaging to a student's self-esteem. It also has serious implications for the institution, where success rates trigger LSC funding and inform the judgements of inspectors. In the first section, the practical issues that can be a problem for adult learners – such as family, financial responsibilities and health – are set in a wider social context so that we can begin to understand why they are such difficult and complex issues to address. We will then go on to look at some of the different practices and interventions that can be used to manage poor punctuality and attendance and improve retention.

Yes, it is challenging, but I am reminded each year in Adult Learners' Week by the students who have achieved their learning goals despite the most difficult personal circumstances that with the right course, support and encouragement almost everyone can make it – and in every case the first person the student thanks for keeping them on track is their lecturer.

Student punctuality and retention as major policy and performance issues

The publication of a number of reports in the early 1990s drew attention to the fact that significant numbers of adult students failed to complete their courses.[1] The drop-out rates were too high and were condemned as a waste of public money. Shortly after this, inspection and funding frameworks were introduced which were designed to give effect to the recommendations contained in these reports.

As a result, organizations whose students do not complete their courses are now penalized financially and their poor performance is made public in inspection reports and success rate performance tables. Similarly, Ofsted and ALI are obsessed with student punctuality, which is generally poor across the sector, as evidenced by analysis of published inspection reports.[2]

Recent LSDA staff surveys have also seen a rise in comments about poor student behaviour, punctuality and attendance.[3] This does not relate only to younger students, although one aspect of lecturers' concerns is that the unreliability of the younger students de-motivates the adult students.

Punctuality and attendance have therefore become key issues for policy-makers, funders, college managers, lecturers and students themselves. The pressures of adult life are no longer an acceptable excuse. As a result, a number of research projects (including Martinez 1995 and McGivney 1996) have been carried out, which identify reasons for poor retention and suggest interventions to address the problem. While the strategies listed at the end of this chapter are aimed at helping you retain your students, do not be satisfied with simple answers or quick fixes. Student retention encompasses a set of complex individual and social issues that also need to be tackled at policy level.

Why don't adult students attend regularly and on time?

Unlike schoolchildren, adult students have chosen to be at college and have probably paid fees, so why are they late for classes and why do they leave courses before completing their studies? Typical responses are:

- 'Students are basically lazy. They like the idea of the course but make excuses rather than efforts.'
- 'Adult students have all sorts of pressures in their lives, it's only to be expected that they attend intermittently and leave before the end of the course.'

There is probably some truth in both these statements, but in order for us to be able to support students and improve performance, we need to dig a bit deeper and to try to understand the deeper social and psychological issues.

Research by the Responsive College Unit Market Research Service has identified the reasons as: 16 per cent financial, 28 per cent personal, 51 per cent course-related and 5 per cent 'other'.[4] However, in my experience, care needs to be taken when interpreting the results of student surveys, or 'official' reasons given by students about their poor attendance or withdrawal from courses. Students will often give a pragmatic response, especially if the lecturer asking them about their non-attendance is the cause of the problem. They are also likely to respond in a way that will protect their self-esteem. As McGivney (1996) has noted, many questionnaires require one box to be ticked, yet the reasons for students' decisions not to finish a course are often complex and relate to the accumulated stress of a number of different issues. The reasons may also be deeply personal and related to their roles and relationships outside college. 'Morag' successfully completed a two-year BTEC Diploma course but had previously dropped out of another course because she had financial and family problems, which added to the pressures of being a student:

> At that point it was just too much. It was too much to read. It was too much to do. It was too much homework. I did small sections of it. I did the study skills, I did women's studies. I didn't do the whole thing. I did psychology as well for a couple of terms, but there was so much of it and there were other things going on as well.

She told the college that she didn't have time to attend and didn't share her personal problems. For some students, it may be the right course but at the wrong time. 'Morag' might have coped with the academic work if her husband had given her emotional and practical support, or if she could have afforded paid domestic help. As with many students, it was everything impacting together that caused her to leave.

'Unable to cope' is a phrase often used by lecturers and students about people who leave courses early, but what does this really mean and is there anything that we could or should do to prevent drop-out? Shortage of money, lack of time or childcare problems appear frequently as reasons both for stress while being a mature student and for leaving courses prematurely (McGivney 1996; Frank and Houghton 1997). While these are very real practical issues, they may have deeper and more complex roots. As already discussed, 'non-traditional' learners who have previously had negative school experiences are likely to have their earlier feelings of inadequacy and failure reinforced. Women students in particular blame themselves more than the college if they 'could not cope' with studying. This is often related to socially constructed notions of gender roles within particular cultures.

The deeper issues are difficult to tackle at an institutional level and consequently responses have tended not to address the problem, but merely cope with the effects.

Physical and mental ill health

Adult students often cite poor health resulting in frequent absences as a reason for not achieving in their initial schooling. Even though their health has improved, they are still managing the psychological effect of 'missing out'. Students may be coping with long-term conditions or new health problems, perhaps caused by ageing or hormonal changes, which affect their concentration in class or their attendance. FE colleges have a legal duty to make reasonable adjustments to cater for disabilities and some long-term health issues, but we need to know about them in order to provide support for them (see Chapter 3).

Poverty and keeping one step ahead of the Department for Work and Pensions

Some external issues that affect students' ability to attend and successfully complete courses arise from social policy, as described by 'Lizzie', one of my students.

> I'm living off income support at the moment. No part-time job earns you enough to be off income support – you end up being more in debt. As soon as you get a job you have to pay your rent totally and not partially and then you have tax. It just becomes horrendous. When I need to buy clay I do the odd bit of sewing which is cash in hand I'm afraid. If I earn a lot I declare it, but if it's only ten or fifteen quid, I don't say anything.

There are students who miss their classes in order to do some casual work to survive. Apart from the absence, the fear of being caught committing benefit fraud is also stressful. As one of my full-time students put it,

> Time and money, there's never enough of either. It's work and your studying suffers, or go on the dole and suffer.

Analysis of research into student withdrawals reveals, unsurprisingly, that unemployed students and those with financial problems were consistently identified as groups with relatively high non-completion rates.[5]

Educational support funds help, but the knock-on effect for students of not having adequate finances is that they cannot afford childcare, travel and decent accommodation, not to mention course materials. This may mean that they cut corners, including going short on food, heat and other essentials. This can affect physical and mental health, cause anxiety and eventually lead to drop-out.

In my own college, I have found that in cases in which students' return to education is motivated by a wish to provide a better life for their children in the future, it is common to have feelings of guilt that they are making their children 'go without' in the present.

Accommodation

Many students find it difficult to find a quiet place to study away from family and noisy neighbours. This is a typical comment:

> The computer is in my children's bedroom so while they are downstairs watching television I'm working away on the computer, but when they go to bed I can't get on with it and I have to write everything by hand if is has to be handed in the next day.

Providing study facilities in college can help some students, but for many mature students with caring commitments, constraints on their time make accessing these places very difficult.

Accommodation can be a major issue for students, especially if they are asylum seekers. For students who become homeless or have significant housing problems during their period of study, this obviously dominates their thoughts and can often result in them leaving their course. College staff may advise on the most appropriate agencies to contact, but this is an area in which there is little more that we can do.

'Accommodation problems' presented by students can often mean far more than housing issues. On further investigation, the problem many turn out to be caused by the breakdown of a relationship with the added trauma that brings, as in this case described to me by one of our college welfare advisers.

> She had been very confident and capable, but her engage-ment broke up in April and she went to pieces. We were writing this letter to get her financial help and she was streaming tears all over it. You could see it was the whole relationship breakdown that had thrown this woman com-pletely upside down. I think he might have been supporting her and there were obvious practical and emotional diffi-culties as she now had no money and was homeless.

From this, we begin to see that although students may be facing 'practical' problems, these may have arisen out of stressful personal situations which affect their ability to cope with college work. Where there is the emotional and practical support of staff and other students, the college may be a lifeline.

At the presentation of awards for outstanding adult learners, a lecturer remarked that it was amazing that some students completed courses despite the string of dreadful things that had occurred in their lives. From my discussions with students, I would suggest that in such circumstances, it may be the positive experience of the course and the support that students find in college relationships that helps them to cope not only with the course but with their lives in general.

External pressures of work and family

For students who are in paid employment, the demands of work can impinge on their study time. There may be the chance of overtime, a change of shift pattern, promotion, seasonal demand, maternity or sick cover. As already mentioned, there are students who rely on casual work (often undeclared) in order to supplement state benefits, and to pay for books, course materials or everyday living expenses.

Many students have families and part-time work as well as attending college. Managing all of these different demands can be physically and emotionally draining.

Students, usually women, who are primary carers may forgo their classes in order to look after a sick relation, take the children to the dentist, the cat to the vet and deal with all the other 'family health' matters, not to mention their own health.[6] It is also unlikely that other family members will take on an increased responsibility for domestic tasks, even when home study is required. Some partners even resort to 'sabotage' by suggesting that the family is suffering from neglect. Guilt is a powerful weapon.

The domestic pressures on lone parents are obviously greater, as college studies make an additional call on time to attend classes and do coursework, and there is no one else with whom to share parenting responsibilities.

These external factors often mean intermittent attendance, which may result in a student getting behind with their work and feeling that they will not be able to catch up and regain their sense of belonging to the course (Cullen 1994). They may also feel embarrassed and guilty about being away and find it difficult to face the lecturer. Apprehension about returning to college after continuity of study is lost often results in withdrawal from a course.

The effects of discontinuity of study can be mitigated if we provide revision or distance and e-learning materials. The problem is that the most vulnerable and hard-pressed students are also those least likely to have the necessary technology at home, or additional time available to come into college to catch up. For a number of students, it would require considerable reorganization of their lives and the cooperation of others, outside college, for them to be able to make use of such college facilities. Morrison's (1992) research found that for women students with families, college time was class contact time. More recently, Janssen (2004) found that adults with caring responsibilities for adult relations rejected e-learning, as they valued the academic and social contact that attending classes provided.

Beyond the practical considerations, education is the source of new ideas. These are not always welcome in the home; for example, the discussion of gender roles and stereotyping in childcare courses could be seen to threaten the power balance between family members. While as providers we may highlight the positive power of education to lead to financial independence, I have had to deal with some very distressed students and irate male relations who do not see this as a good thing.

The college experience as a contributory factor in non-completion

The prevalence of non-academic factors among the reasons that mature students give for leaving courses early could lead to colleges being complacent about their services. Certainly, colleges have been slow to consider that retention might be linked to a bad classroom experience, probably partly as a result of the reluctance of students to give lecturers negative feedback and the tendency for some students to blame themselves for the situation.

Under-achievement and drop-out has often been linked to a deficiency in the student, such as poor study skills, lack of ability, home pressures or lack of commitment. However, research into student retention in FE indicates that the quality of teaching and learning is a significant factor (Martinez 1995, 1997). This is supported by analysis of inspection reports on adult provision, which identifies the narrow range of teaching methods, some poor resources and insufficient feedback to learners on their progress as key weaknesses across the sector.[7]

Often, insufficient thought is given to the way students feel about themselves as learners, their experiences and concerns and their preferred learning styles. Educationalists have been more concerned with the problems that students bring to them than with the problems that educational institutions may be responsible for creating. We have often failed to understand the complexity and inter-relatedness of the issues facing mature students. By looking at the student and not the person, we forget that for mature students, 'education is squeezed in at the margins of life' (Alan Tuckett, NIACE).

Different value systems can be discerned within the complexity of providing education today. Colleges have to manage the tension between meeting students' needs (and thereby retaining students) and meeting the narrow requirements of funding bodies. Students have to find ways to skill and empower themselves within an education system which still privileges white, male, able-bodied, heterosexual values, despite efforts by institutions to embrace equality and diversity. However, as practitioners we should not let this depress us, because being aware of the issues brings us part-way to resolving them.

Lack of confidence and stress

Some students have so little self-confidence that they believe the only reason they have been given a place on a course is that the college made a mistake, or failed to spot their weaknesses. One student told me how she nearly dropped out before she had even started the course.

I thought of not coming after I was accepted on the course ... I suppose there's fear of failure, isn't there ... I didn't want to go to college about three or four weeks before. I said 'I'm only doing this because there's nothing else for me to do, I don't want to do it' ... I couldn't understand it. I'd been looking forward to the interview. I'd come and got a place and suddenly it was really strange. I think you have to work through that and the way I did it was to say I'll give it a month and if I don't like it, I'll leave, but of course in that time I came here and I loved it.

This sort of 'lack of confidence' that students may feel is often a fear that they are entering an alien environment in which their working-class background, or ethnic identity, singles them out as being different or 'lacking' (Reay 1996). The range of concerns is well illustrated by the following extract from an essay by an Access course student:

When I joined the course, one of my greatest worries was what kind of tutors would I have? I had heard of many cases where tutors would enter the class and deliver their knowledge brusquely and then walk out. My fears were unfounded in this case, as at the end of every lecture there is tutorial time to discuss in private any problem arising from the subject just learnt. The second worry I had was to do with the reactions of other students to me and how would I cope if any of them made a racist remark to me. I was so glad that such a case never arose! Everyone has treated me very well. My third worry was academically related. After twelve years without having had any formal education, my greatest fear was that I had become 'antique' and as such I might not be able to take in new ideas and concepts.

Lack of confidence and stress are words that arise again and again in conversations with staff and students. Some students remain anxious, often concerned that they will be publicly humiliated about what they do not know, or cannot do, as they may have been in the past. We need to be careful not to misinterpret an unconfident student's reluctance to contribute in class as lack of understanding or interest. The following student comment is typical:

It's fear of failure. If I go back to the first day, in a huge room with people you don't know ... You don't feel at ease to talk out in the class. When you have to stand up and give your first presentation, that's so nerve-racking, you can hear your voice and you're shaking with nerves.

We also need to understand behaviour within a cultural framework. A student's reluctance to contribute or to challenge the views of others in class may not be an indicator of low personal confidence so much as behaviour within a cultural norm: for example, within some Muslim families, women are expected to take a passive role (Afshar 1994).

It is sometimes difficult for a student to hear or own positive feedback because of the effects of negative feedback from school or family over a long period. Difficulty in owning intellectual skills is also deeply embedded within working-class identity (Bhavnani 1993; Luttrell 1993; Reay 1996). By giving students regular, developmental feedback on their learning (Chapter 8) and referring them to support services (Chapter 7), we can help them gain in confidence and self-esteem.

Loss of confidence, exhaustion and overload can be felt by any student at some time during their course. Seasonal factors often don't help. We all know that attendance drops and students hit a 'flat spot' around November and February, when winter illnesses, dark evenings and bad weather combine with the uphill academic struggle – a long journey only just under way. Another key time is the summer, when examinations and anxiety about the future are issues. Some students certainly suffer from examination phobia, and research links some late withdrawals from courses to this (McGivney 1996).

Thankfully, these negative spells usually pass quickly and are followed by phases of elation and achievement. By being vigilant and following up quickly, with perhaps tutorial, mentoring or peer group activities, we can help people get through a difficult patch and prevent withdrawal. There is nothing like feeling that people care about you and believe in your capabilities to raise the spirits. Although for part-time students with outside commitments there may be limited opportunities to integrate into the social life of the institution, we can organize social events and use strategies such as 'study buddies' to encourage cohesion.

Fear of success

Strange as it may sound, there are students who are worried about being successful. While students may tell us that they want education to help them change their lives, they may also be anxious that gaining a qualification and starting a new career will alter their status and separate them from their friends and family in an elitist way (Edwards 1993; McGivney 1996). Notions of equality shape relationships with friends (Allan 1989). Education may alter one person's status in relation to another, which may create a tension, as issues of hierarchy and authority are introduced into a relationship which has grown out of similarity rather than difference. When education has brought about intellectual growth in an individual, which has not been shared by his or her partner, it may lead to a re-evaluation of the relationship with negative results – what I call the '*Educating Rita* effect'. At the heart of this is class. Educational success is also a challenge to authenticity and social group identity (Reay 1996). Thus, some students may feel very isolated in their attempts to manage personal change and meet all the different demands made on them by lecturers, their family and friends. Social mobility enabled by education is a double-edged sword.

The control of knowledge and communicating respect for cultural identity

The classroom is a microcosm of the power relationships in the wider society. If a student does not feel that his or her intellectual beliefs and values are consistent with the academic norms and conventions of the class and college, then there is a high risk that this will lead to non-integration and perhaps withdrawal. We need more than positive marketing and practical improvements, such as the provision of prayer rooms and physical access for people with disabilities, to make adults from a breadth of social groups feel that they 'belong' in the college. We need to ensure that the programme content and delivery values the range of experience and concerns that students bring. Developing a curriculum from the multiple experiences of adult students is a challenge. The non-award-bearing traditions of adult education offered possibilities for the curriculum to be negotiated with students, but the increasing emphasis on conforming to external pressures, including those of accrediting bodies, has reduced these opportunities. External demands now make the democratization of the classroom, and any shift of control over knowledge from teacher to students, far more difficult to achieve. There would appear, though, to be greater scope to explore issues of equality and diversity within the expressive arts and humanities than within the more narrowly focused vocational routes and competence-based curriculum. Some significant and successful work with disempowered groups, including prostitutes and people in prison, has been done through painting, dance and music, where differences and continuities of experience have been made visible through some very powerful self-devised statements.[8]

We need to recognize the existence of differential power within the classroom. It affects whose voice is heard and whose experience is valued. It controls the production of knowledge and the maintenance of inequalities. As described earlier, adult students have already learnt, through their previous experiences of education, the ways in which social codes such as race and gender impact on behaviour within classrooms. The choices students make about what they study and the anxieties they feel about entering a classroom have a relationship to their position of power relative to the lecturer and other students. Thus, a woman enrolling in a 'traditional male subject', such as plumbing, may not only feel disadvantaged by her lack of technical knowledge, but also that she will have to cope with a 'male culture' and possibly sexist behaviour. Research, including that of Bhavnani (1993), Luttrell (1993) and Reay (1996), has revealed the tensions experienced by working-class people in identifying themselves as both working class and 'intelligent'.

This means that while many students are attempting to improve their life chances, they also have to manage the stress of functioning in an alien world – 'coping' means attempting to relate to the teaching and learning style and also epistemological issues about whose knowledge and culture is being passed on. Students wish to have their skills acknowledged, their cultures and contributions valued. If we fail to achieve this, then people from socially disadvantaged groups will continue to leave our courses.

Time pressures linked to drop-out are not as simple as they appear

Time pressures have been consistently identified as an issue for adult students (including Mansell and Parkin 1990; Morrison 1992). However, some curriculum responses show little understanding of the way some people's time is constrained. For example, for women students, 'time' is linked to the practical issues of fitting classes around their caring commitments, but is also linked to the way society sees women's roles. For many women, giving time to people and time received is linked to caring and being valued. So, for many female students, attending their class is important, as it is time for their own development. Finding other students and staff who are interested in them as people as well as students makes coming to college special, and student feedback often shows appreciation of the time that staff give them. The reverse experience can therefore be received as 'not caring'. Mansell and Parkin's (1990) study found that among the aspects that withdrawn part-time FE students had found unsatisfactory was that they had not had enough time to discuss problems related to their study, and found the college impersonal. Edwards' (1993) study of women in higher education found that students felt staff should be enthusiastic and committed to sharing their knowledge with students. They should make time for them and not give them the impression that they would rather be doing something else![9] In my view 'time management' is as much about dealing with feelings about how time is used as with its physical apportionment.

If getting students to attend regularly and punctually and complete their studies were easy, we would have sorted it out by now. However, as the senior manager in a college with 25,000 adult students, I know that some curriculum teams are more consistently successful than others. In what follows, I will draw out the approaches and strategies that have worked in my own college and across the sector more widely.

Why poor punctuality needs to be challenged and managed

It is inevitable that a student is late once in a while because of circumstances beyond their control – but there are persistent offenders and this needs dealing with. As I have just detailed, adult students have responsibilities, which include: dropping off and picking up children from school; looking after elderly and sick relatives; shift and night work. They may have health problems themselves, need to sign on or go for a job interview, wait until after a certain time to get cheap transport and, with evening classes, they may get held up leaving work or by poor transport. They may have lost or never acquired the habit of good timekeeping and reliability.

However, on further investigation, you will probably find that those who are punctual also have time pressures – but manage them.

In my experience many lecturers come to expect their students to be late, and therefore instead of dealing with the lateness they 'work round it'. Responses include: starting the class later; moaning at those who are on time; starting the class on time but then breaking off to update each arrival; and stating that it is a 'workshop' and that as each student has their own learning plan it's OK. Well, it's not OK, and this is why:

- it is disrespectful to the lecturer and other students
- it is disruptive to others' learning
- it can damage an individual's acceptance into the group, as other students perceive lateness as discourteous
- it is a bad habit that will not be tolerated in the workplace
- it sets a lax tone, which can lead to a general malaise

- you will probably end up doing a catch-up with late-comers during your break and not be fresh for the next class.

If your organization has a system for managing student punctuality you should use it, but here are some ideas.

Ways to manage punctuality

Do

- Start as you mean to go on at the first session. Set high standards – having high expectations of students is a characteristic of successful colleges (Ofsted).
- Late slips – you quietly hand it to the student, who has to complete and return it, the theory being that they then reflect on whether it was necessary to be late.
- Ask for an apology to the class in the target language, if it is a foreign language class or ESOL.
- Contracts that clearly state standards of behaviour and are signed by students can be referred back to when formal action may be required for persistent lateness. Pre-written contracts are often used for vocational courses. Levels of punctuality and attendance are made explicit and usually linked to the standards of performance required to gain the qualification or employer requirements. It may be preferable in other types of course for the class to draw up their own contract at the first meeting. This allows students to say what they expect of the lecturer and from each other and allows the lecturer to say what is expected of students. As this is collectively negotiated, it can be more powerful and appropriate for adult students. It needs to be printed, circulated to students and adhered to! Issues to be discussed include the importance of lessons starting on time and what late-comers should do.
- Exclude from the lesson/part of the lesson – this sounds risky when you are trying to get people to turn up, but I have known it work well with Access courses. Some practical classes allow a late student to attend and

observe or assist other students, but not to do their own practical work.

- Start every class on time, or the ones who do make the effort won't bother in the future.
- Always start with something unmissable.
- Consider incentives, e.g. book tokens or art materials, for the most punctual student.
- Be in the classroom on time yourself – not down the corridor photocopying or talking to a colleague.
- Always note lateness and follow up after the class or in tutorials. Make speedy referrals to welfare services where appropriate.

Take care

- Disorganization can be a symptom of dyslexia or other specific learning difficulty – this student may need help with organization and time management.
- Lateness may be a reflection of lack of confidence to say to family or employer, 'I have to go to my class now.' Assertiveness training might be helpful.

Don't

- Ignore lateness – always challenge it.
- Indulge in ritual, public humiliation of latecomers.
- Rant to the students who attend class on time about the others who have not turned up.

You may need a variety of strategies for different situations. Something that works well for a full-time course based on practical skills, such as salon days for beauty therapy NVQ students, may not be appropriate for an A-level evening class.

If students have an acceptable reason for not being able to start at the beginning of your class, such as nursery opening times, it may be possible to negotiate a later start, depending on the subject: but this new arrangement must be adhered to.[10]

Discussing lateness with students

Whatever the reason for lateness, you need to deal with it in an adult-to-adult manner, not a parent-to-child style.[11] You are trying to help the student take responsibility for his or her own actions and be respectful to yourself and the other students. Always discuss it in private.

Every school pupil knows there are lessons you can be late for and others you cannot, and it is not just because they are run by a teacher with the methods of a boot camp sergeant. You will find that with the same group of students, some lecturers get better punctuality than others – I firmly believe that you can make a difference.

Managing student absence

When a student's attendance is intermittent your alarm bells should start to ring. Tom Wayman's poem 'Did I Miss Anything?' is a reflection on student absence that we can all connect with.

Did I Miss Anything?
Tom Wayman

Question frequently asked by
students after missing a class

Nothing. When we realized you weren't here
we sat with our hands folded on our desks
in silence, for the full two hours

Everything. I gave an exam worth
40 per cent of the grade for this term
and assigned some reading due today
on which I'm about to hand out a quiz
worth 50 per cent

Nothing. None of the content of this course
has value or meaning
Take as many days off as you like:
any activities we undertake as a class
I assure you will not matter either to you or me
and are without purpose

Everything. A few minutes after we began last time
a shaft of light descended and an angel
or other heavenly being appeared
and revealed to us what each woman or man must do
to attain divine wisdom in this life and
the hereafter
This is the last time the class will meet
before we disperse to bring this good news to all people
on earth

Nothing. When you are not present
how could something significant occur?

Everything. Contained in this classroom
is a microcosm of human existence
assembled for you to query and examine and ponder
This is not the only place such an opportunity has been
gathered

but it was one place

and you weren't here.

from *Did I Miss Anything? Selected Poems 1973–1993* (Madeira Park, BC: Harbour)

Intermittent attendance often turns into withdrawal from the course because students do not feel that they will be able to catch up on missed work. It is important that students who may be having difficulties are identified quickly and offered support. If they have concerns with the course, they may prefer to speak with someone other than their lecturer.

We need to be sensitive and always discuss the matter in private – you never know what might be revealed. I had one student who was physically abused by her partner and did not come into college on the days when the bruising was noticeable.

Attendance problems may indicate a mismatch of expectations, either the student of him or herself or the institution, or the lecturer of the students. It may be helpful to remind yourself of the issues discussed in Chapter 1.

Strategies to improve retention

Flexible and modular course design as a response to time pressures

The type of curriculum that suits adult students was discussed in Chapter 2. Modular programmes and e-learning centres have been suggested as one way of better meeting the learning needs of adults whose lives are time-poor and unpredictable. While it is positive that a student who can no longer attend a course at a particular time can transfer to a different mode, that student has lost some key anchors and motivators by not having a group learning experience. An isolated and fragmented learning experience can be the negative side of 'flexible programming'. Support structures and group work needs to be maintained to keep students motivated.

For students with low self-esteem, 'flexibility' can be permission not to attend. For students who find it difficult to find time for themselves, the expectation of regular attendance is helpful: 'not letting down the group or the lecturer' is part of giving themselves permission to have personal time and allows them to control any feelings of guilt and 'selfishness'.

Seeing the whole person

Most students would have a more positive experience of returning to education, and colleges would improve their retention rates, if there were a more holistic approach to the educational process. All aspects of students' lives influence and are influenced by their return to college, and this should be recognized in programming and delivery.

> The pressure of juggling the roles of student, partner, worker, would be lessened if the role of student was seen as including, not excluding, the others. (Cullen 1994: 8)

Creating an adult learning community

Students need to feel welcome and that they belong to the group and institution. Social interaction assists the learning process and encourages students to attend regularly. Even though many adult students have outside commitments that mean that their time in college is focused on teaching and learning, there is a need to provide some social space. A base room is particularly important when a college has a majority of younger students. Other adult-focused facilities include a crèche and car parking. All facilities and equipment also need to meet adult expectations regarding comfort and cleanliness. Social activities with an adult focus at class and institutional level promote a sense of 'belonging'. They also give students something to look forward to, and we all like that. Often lecturers arrange course-related activities such as theatre trips or an end-of-term meal in a restaurant. An active Students' Association can be invaluable for bringing students together for interaction and mutual support, although it may need staff encouragement and support to get students involved.

Good communications can really help to make students feel part of an organization. These may be college-wide, such as a student newsletter or website, but the personal touch is always appreciated. I always used to send my students a New Year card reminding them of the date of the first class in January, with something tantalizing about activities for the new term. It was always appreciated and I had a full class at the start of term. Students with periods off for sickness also benefit from contact.

Peer group support is a most powerful aid to retaining students. It can be encouraged in a number of ways, including group learning activities, mentor schemes, study circles, volunteers to support students with disabilities, pairing students up for conversation exchange (ESOL students and modern foreign languages students), and car lift schemes.

Teaching and learning
Adult students respond to teaching that recognizes their concerns and aspirations: for example, research shows that courses that include a block of work experience have a relatively low withdrawal rate. Adults expect lecturers to be passionate about their subject and they thrive in stimulating learning environments in which their previous experience and knowledge is recognized and valued. An in-depth understanding of equality and diversity has to be at the heart of teaching and learning (see Chapter 3). Good relationships between staff and students hold the group together and enhance learning. If a part-time student

is having problems that are affecting his or her ability to study, he or she will often prefer to talk to the lecturer than to an unknown counsellor. It is therefore important that as lecturers we are approachable, as well as good teachers. However, we need clear boundaries and should never attempt to take on the welfare role ourselves.

Monitoring attendance and punctuality should be an integral part of student guidance and support, and effective tutorials are at the heart of this. Personal tutorials are the time when individual progress and course-related issues are discussed. Regular feedback, both written and verbal, which includes suggestions about ways to improve performance, are a key to students having a sense of their own achievement and remaining motivated. Fitting regular one-to-one review and action-planning into part-time courses can be difficult, but is essential.

Support services

Colleges provide a range of student support services (see Chapter 7), and it is important that we keep up to date on what they are and how our students can access them. We don't need to be experts ourselves, but we do need to promote the services and, most importantly, follow up on referrals.

How we can help our students complete their courses

- Develop a professional relationship of trust that does not cause stress to either party. We need to see our students as whole people, but to avoid getting over-involved in their personal lives. Always refer non-academic problems to a professional and never give students a home telephone number for 'emergencies'.
- Take early action to help students who are under-achieving, missing sessions or showing signs of stress.
- Keep up to date on support services and always follow up on any referrals.
- Know alternative courses or modes of study, including e-learning packages, and how to transfer students who can no longer attend a class because of external

circumstances. (However, these options do not suit all students.)

- Encourage students to support each other with academic work 'study buddies'.
- Talk through with students how they might elicit practical help from family and friends.
- Treat adult students as adults and as equals.
- Be approachable and show genuine interest. Listen to students' problems and anxieties and acknowledge them rather than minimizing them.
- When discussing poor attendance, don't take the first response as the real reason. Give space for further disclosure, without prying.
- Remember, a student who tells us they are thinking of leaving the course may really be looking for help to continue.
- Talk to colleagues about the strategies they use and share the best – remembering that not all strategies work in all situations.
- If a student really cannot continue, see what can be done to credit them with partial achievement, or suggest some visual or written record of their progress. This way, they are taking a 'learning break' rather than dropping out, which prepares the way for a return in the future and maintains self-esteem.

Is this a battle we can win?

Many colleges set targets for punctuality and attendance within their quality assurance systems and report on them in their self assessment report. It is likely that college managers will monitor this through data and classroom observations. Inspectors certainly will!

It is important that we use feedback from students at course and college level to improve services, not just in the end-of-course review but throughout the year. If students see that staff are prepared to change something in response to feedback, this always has a positive impact.

Effective practice relies on leadership from senior staff, and coordinated learner services from first contact to completion, but the greatest influence on student punctuality and completion is the degree to which students respect their lecturers for their professionalism and humanity. In order to help our diverse student population to succeed, we need to avail ourselves of every opportunity to refresh our subject expertise and enthusiasm and improve our teaching skills. Be pro-active, whether it is work-shadowing in industry, attending a course, observing experienced and successful lecturers, or any other developmental activity.

In the end, we can only do our best. If a student leaves, it is often a disappointment to him or her and us, especially if a great deal of support has been given: but sometimes it may be, as a college counsellor suggests, that students are 'looking for something in courses that cannot be found'. Encourage a student who really cannot continue to see it as a learning break and to return when personal circumstances permit.

Notes

[1]   *Student Completion Rates in Further Education* (DES 1991), *Measuring Up: Performance Indicators in Further Education* (SOED/HMI 1992) and *Unfinished Business* (Audit Commission/Ofsted, 1993).

[2]   See ALI and Ofsted websites.

[3]   The 2002 survey was based on the comments from 13,000 respondents from 100 FE colleges. The comments about attendance and punctuality were the sixth most frequent response to the question, 'What would make your job better?'

[4]   These results were for all students, not just adults.

[5]   McGivney (1996), Hayes (1999).

[6]   Janssen's (2004) research describes the pressure of being an adult student while caring for an elderly relation.

[7]   Richard Moore, ALI inspector, reporting key findings at the Central London Learning Partnership Conference, May 2005.

[8]   Examples of successful practice include the work of Dance United with women prisoners and Second Wave (see the box on page 56).

[9]   The culture shock of transferring from the supportive environment of an Access course to a higher education institution has been cited as a reason for withdrawal of these students from their degree courses (Moore 1995).

[10] In workshop-based courses such as NVQ hairdressing or beauty therapy, where the salon is running a commercial service that includes evenings and weekends, it may be possible to agree a later 'shift' for some students, but the timing of taught sessions remains fixed.

[11] This refers to Transactional Analysis, which is a human interaction theory based on three ego states (parent, adult, child) that affect communication. Transactional Analysis was founded by Eric Berne in the 1960s and is still being developed today. It has wide applications in clinical, therapeutic, organizational and personal development.

7 Supporting adult learners

The Adult Learning Inspectorate (ALI) has found that support for students is a strength of the provision they have inspected in the learning and skills sector. However, they have also commented that specialist support services often operate at the wrong times or in the wrong locations to meet the needs of adult students.

Just because students are adults does not mean that they are able to cope with the academic and personal aspects of returning to study any more easily than younger students. As discussed in Chapter 6, unlike most younger students, adults have to fit study around the demands of families and often employers. For adults, the college part of doing a course is the tip of the iceberg – the mass is the part that is outside the classroom.

In this chapter, we will consider the most appropriate ways to support the learning and emotional needs of adult students. First, I will suggest the overall approach that we should take; we will go on to look at specific points in the learner journey through the college or other learning centre.

A holistic approach to supporting learners

Adult students need to weave learning into already complex lives. Being a student is not confined to the taught hours and coursework: reading, visits to the theatre or art galleries, field trips and work placement all impinge on the rest of their lives. For colleges to ignore this is not helpful to the student.

I therefore advocate what I call 'a holistic approach' to student support. This approach considers the whole experience of the student, which means that we plan course-related activities in relation to the organization of our students' lives and provide practical and emotional support to help them adjust to the changes that will undoubtedly take place over the duration of their studies. However, this way of working does not mean that boundaries between the public and private aspects of individuals' lives are breached. It must be up to each student to decide to what extent they wish to separate or connect the different aspects of their lives. Some students' coping strategies rely on separating the worlds of home, work and college; for others, combining them is more helpful (Edwards 1993).

Although colleges have student support staff who provide a range of services (see the box on page 103), the key person to whom students look to provide support, certainly in the first instance, is the lecturer/tutor. This is because if they have problems students want to talk to someone they know and trust. In addition, when students are already having difficulties, finding a moment to go and see someone else and explain their needs is one more pressure. As lecturers we are the people who observe interactions in the class, monitor learning progress and spot when one of our students is not happy or not achieving.

Lecturers may not feel qualified to discuss anything other than academic issues with their students (Munn et al. 1992; Moore 1995), yet it becomes difficult to give academic support if the wider context of a student's life is not taken into consideration. (This does not preclude referral to other individuals and support agencies).

How should support be managed? Munn et al. (1992) found that students had high satisfaction rates with courses in which educational guidance and support were integral to the design of the course. Their findings were that mature students make little use of college-wide provision, especially if it means making a special journey. They may also feel that there is a stigma attached to seeking additional help if it is seen as 'bolt-on provision for non-copers' (Deere et al. 1997), rather than 'open-door' support to which they are entitled. However, Mansell and Parkin (1990) found that part-time students who felt they had limited access to teaching resented time being taken up with learning support.

As discussed in Chapter 6, the importance of lecturers being pro-active and taking early action to help students who are under-achieving, missing sessions or showing signs of stress cannot be over-emphasized. We should not wait for students to ask for help. Often adult students do not want to highlight that they are having problems and do not ask for help even if it is available, particularly if they think that it may support patho-logizing discourses about working-class or minority ethnic students. We also need to remember that some adults have spent years trying to cover up their lack of skills and knowledge and have not admitted, even to themselves, that they have a learning disability. The senior counsellor at my college confirms that a supportive relationship between students and lecturers is a key success factor:

> If they stick with their courses it usually means that they've had a very encouraging tutor, and what has happened in two cases that I can think of is that these students have finally been able to acknowledge what they needed, which is amazing, rather than going on covering it up.

Identifying support needs and promoting available services

It is important that special support needs are identified as early as possible. This means ensuring that if a student declares him or herself to have a disability or learning difficulty on the appli-cation or enrolment forms, this is communicated to the staff who will interview the student and to the course director and lecturers. As obvious as this sounds, systems are not always as efficient as they should be.

Many colleges now do initial screening to identify areas in which students will require support, especially with lan-guage, literacy and numeracy. However, even with systems in place to make an early identification of support needs, some students' needs will not be picked up until they arrive in our class. We need to know where to refer students, but, most especially, we need to talk to students and support staff to prepare the way and then make sure that our referral has been followed up. We then need to maintain good communications with learning support staff. This ensures that the work they are doing with students is relevant to the course. We can also find out ways to adjust our teaching to better meet the needs of these students. For example, for dyslexic students, it may be helpful to accept some work on video or audio tape/CD and to write key or technical words on the board to aid note-taking. For more strategies for working with students with disabilities see the box on page 41.

Even if students are given a handbook with a statement of entitlement along with a list of support services and contact details, nothing is as good as meeting the people. If you can get members of the learner services team to visit your class so that they can explain what support they can provide, it can be really helpful. It is not just about knowing what the services are, it is about beginning to develop a relationship of trust. Most of us have had bad experiences accessing services at some time and the stereotype of patronizing officialdom needs to be blown away.

Induction

I have found it useful to treat induction as a process rather than a single event, introducing information or activities such as a demonstration of the computer Intranet (e-learning materials including course notes and revision materials for missed sessions) over the first month. There are always students who start courses late, or who miss a session, so an induction checklist is a helpful way of ensuring that all students receive key information about your course and institution-wide services.

College support services

General information – available at reception, by e-mail and telephone. Some organizations have evening and weekend help lines or use a call centre.

Additional learning support (ALS) – a funding stream for any additional support required to enable the learner to achieve their primary learning goal. This can include literacy,

---

numeracy and language (but not for those on SfL programmes), support for any disability or learning difficulty
(dyslexia, Asperger's, hearing and sight impairment,
behavioural difficulties, mental health etc). Must be based
on clearly identified learning needs that affect the individual, not the whole class.

Chaplaincy – new multi-faith service provided in some FE
colleges from 2006.

Childcare – may be an on-site nursery or advice and
financial support to find a suitable childminder or nursery.

Counselling – may include help with emotional, practical or
motivational problems at home, college or work, or a
combination of these.

Educational advice and careers guidance – from an independent
expert, available at times convenient to adult learners, to
help them identify the most appropriate course and future
career path. Some institutions offer evening as well as
daytime drop-in sessions.

Elder care – very little outside special projects. Contact
NIACE, Older & Bolder for further information.

Examinations/assessment preparation – provided in-course
(individual or whole group) or via additional modules.
Sheltered examination conditions are helpful for some
nervous students. Revision workshops reinforce learning
and can increase confidence.

Financial advice and support – about grants from charitable
trusts (for current study or progress to higher education).
Includes explanation about regulations relating to social
benefits and study and can refer or liaise with external
agencies. An Adult Learning Grant (applicable to level 2
entitlement students) is planned for introduction in 2006/
2007).

Job search/volunteering – sometimes available via notice-boards, but may be through personal contacts in vocational areas where there are established links with employers.

Learner support funds – 'at the discretion of college' but basically materials, equipment, childcare and travel for people over 19. In all cases focusing on priority groups (low income, single parents, skills for life).

Pastoral support – with adults, likely to be part of the course tutor role, with referral to other services.

Students with disabilities or learning difficulties – a range of services and equipment provided under ALS (see above). Good networks of specialist organizations for additional advice and practical help.

Study skills – note-taking, essay-writing, effective use of library and study centres, available on the course or via additional modules, rolling programmes or drop-in sessions.

Travel – may be financial support or local schemes such as a free bus service (especially beneficial in rural areas).

Make sure you know the referral process for all these services and if your organization has gaps, for example, lack of access to services in the evenings, then raise the issue with management.

Tutorials and supporting academic work

It is important that all students, including part-timers, have regular timetabled opportunities to discuss their academic progress with a tutor – not end-of-class or corridor conversations. In some circumstances ALS can pay for planned, additional tutorial time. The management of feedback is discussed in Chapter 8.

The 'key tutor' – role model, mentor and advocate

When I was researching the factors that helped students who might otherwise have dropped out of their courses, I developed the concept of the 'key tutor'. This is not an actual job, but is the support role provided by someone who is usually, but not necessarily, a member of staff. Sometimes this person is officially designated to the support role, but often they take it on informally. McGivney also identified people carrying out this important role:

> All the evidence indicates that good staff–student interaction is one of the keys to good retention rates ... many have found that it is often informal contact and rapport with a staff member – not necessarily a counsellor or a personal tutor or even someone with a formal pastoral role – that gives students the encouragement to continue studying. The key attributes of such a person are friendliness, availability and interest in the student. (McGivney 1996: 133)

Smith and Bailey (1993) agree that it is important for students to have sufficient good-quality contact with staff if they are to complete courses successfully, and they link personal attention with good retention rates. Cullen (1994) found in her research that students wanted to be listened to and have their problems and anxieties acknowledged by lecturers, rather than minimized. Munn et al. (1992) identified the importance to students of being treated as equals, with tutors being approachable and displaying genuine interest in them.

These 'key tutors' have a depth of understanding about what it means to be a mature student, often based on personal experience; they are role models and mentors. They see beyond what is presented, they are pro-active and demonstrate real interest in their students. Students appreciate this and are aware of staff attitudes. They appreciate the extra time that many lecturers give them beyond the official class times, and are increasingly aware of the demands that are made on staff, although there are clearly issues of differential power within the relationship and boundaries concerning privacy that need to be respected.

Maria is always very busy. That's not saying anything bad, but she's always so stressed out. She's got so much on that she hasn't got time to talk to her students a lot, so she doesn't know her students as well as she could. Sandra really knows her students well. She always seems to make time for them and she's sensitive when they've got problems, even when they don't say anything.

It is important that our students feel that there is someone who will listen to them and that there are actions that can be taken to resolve problems. Moore (1995) and McGivney (1996) have both highlighted the number of students who leave courses without discussing their reasons with staff. Perhaps they do not believe that anyone is interested in them, or that anything can be done to help them, particularly if it is not an academic problem that is preventing them from studying. When students do tell us that they are going to have to leave the course, experience suggests that they are looking for help to continue. Sometimes it is practical help that is needed, but often it becomes a need for emotional support.

I need to emphasize here that lecturers and students need to respect each other and develop a professional relationship that does not cause stress to either of them. We should never get personally involved in students' domestic or welfare issues. Always refer such matters to the professionals. Also beware of being taken advantage of with academic work, such as offering extra sessions when a student has fallen behind (unless this is part of ALS) or giving your home telephone number for telephone tutorials. I have known of situations where students have misunderstood a human response to their support needs in an unfortunate way, resulting in unwanted telephone calls at home and, in the saddest case, stalking. Be warm, but have clear boundaries. Women lecturers in particular can end up giving a lot of extra 'gift time' to students who are struggling, sometimes because college resources have been cut back (James and Diment 2003). Do not let management take advantage of your wish to see your students do well or have expectations that, if you are a woman, you will 'naturally' engage in the emotional labour of supporting students with personal issues.

Study skills and time management

Taking a holistic approach to support is not a 'soft option'. For example, if students are informed of deadlines for assignments in good time so that they can plan research and writing into their lives outside the class, then those deadlines should be met, except in extreme circumstances. Students have told me that although they appreciate being treated as adults and autonomous learners, they also quite like lecturers 'getting tough' about deadlines. Saying we have our own deadline to meet for an assessment gives them 'permission' to prioritize their time over the demands of others at home and work and not let us down.

This highlights that the effective apportionment of time is more complex than it may seem, and to help our students we need to dig a bit deeper than responding with 'they need a time management course'. First, the inability to organize belongings and course notes and prioritize workload can be a symptom of a specific learning difficulty such as dyslexia.[1] It does not necessarily imply laziness or the inability to 'get down to it'. Second, research indicates that women students have a tendency to prioritize others' needs above their own as a result of social conditioning: 'taking time for study, in the main, was viewed as taking time for themselves and therefore taking it away from others' (Edwards 1993). Study plans and routines assume control over time, yet people with families have reduced control over the way their time is spent. Study and family responsibilities are both task-related, rather than clock-related, so there is no set amount of time that can be planned for their fulfilment. The study skill that some students, especially women, may find most useful is assertiveness training, as this helps them to consider their own needs as learners and 'give themselves permission' to say no to others' demands on them.

While there is undoubtedly a need to help students who have been away from education to refresh their skills in writing discursive prose, using libraries effectively and developing note-taking and problem-solving skills, I have some concerns that the pressures mature students find themselves under are attributed to the poor management of their time, rather than unequal life opportunities. Bargh *et al.* (1994) are among the researchers who have concluded that mature students with complex lives are in fact skilled time managers.

Support from peers, family and friends

The emotional and practical support of other students, or ex-students, is extremely helpful and we need to find as many ways as possible to encourage this, whether it is through mentoring, study circles, group assignments or social events. Successful examples of peer support and mentoring are described by Champney *et al.* (2005).

Families and friends are not always willing or able to be supportive. If a student's relations have not obtained qualifications themselves, it is difficult for them to help, as they do not have experience of study at this level. There may even be jealousy or emotional sabotage (Hayes 1999). Students' own feelings of guilt about neglecting their families can also hinder achievement: for example, Morrison (1992) found that the outwardly passive thinking and reading times, which we tend to ask students to do at home, are easily eroded by family demands. Students can also feel guilty about what they see as 'reduced standards', especially if other family members are critical of eating convenience foods or having to do their own ironing.

On the other hand, families can be wonderfully supportive – especially older children, who are studying themselves and can empathize. Students on vocational courses such as catering and beauty therapy often find friends and neighbours are happy to have the kids for a while in exchange for a manicure or a sample of haute cuisine!

Note

[1] Excellent guidance for study skills can be found on www.dylexia-teacher.com

8 Recognizing achievement and recording progression

A sense of achievement is very important to adult students, but having this recorded on a certificate is not necessarily a priority.[1] Having said that, people with qualifications should not underestimate the significance that gaining even a basic level qualification may have for someone who until now has 'failed' in the eyes of the education system. This is clear in the reactions of one of my students, who came to college with no qualifications and low self-esteem, and progressed in time to higher education:

> I was desperate to pass my GCSE maths and English and I struggled all year. I was so nervous and I was so impatient for the results. I phoned the examinations officer. He told me the results and I was screaming. I put the phone down and I was jumping for joy and then I rang everybody and told them – then when you get the certificates to prove that you can actually do it, it makes you feel good.

In this chapter, I define achievement in its broadest terms within non-accredited and qualifications courses. It includes: the development of knowledge, skills and attitudes; the practical application of that knowledge outside the classroom and the impact on others; improved self-esteem and confidence, personal development that allows an individual to take on new roles; and progression into employment or further learning. We should not forget that achievement covers a wide spectrum of human endeavour. For some students, achievement will be gaining sufficient Access credits to progress to higher education: for others, attending class regularly or working cooperatively with other students may be a significant advance. There are also student situations in which achievement is not about gaining ground, it is about not losing it.

The language we use to discuss achievement often becomes very technical: progress, progression, attainment, formative and summative assessment, measuring learning outcomes against objectives.[2] At an inspection meeting, I experienced a misunderstanding about whether the 'lack of progression' referred to was students' poor achievement on the course, or the fact that a number of them had not moved on to the next level of study. If we do not always understand the meaning of terms, or have a shared use of them with other professionals, how confusing is it for our students when we ask them to self-assess their learning, or when we give them feedback?

Whether we are teaching qualification- or non-qualification-bearing courses, our students need to know that they are learning, as well as enjoying their studies. It is worth remembering that one of the reasons that students drop out of courses is because they do not have a sense that they are getting anywhere.

Qualification-bearing courses

If you are teaching a course that is examined or validated by an external organization such as City and Guilds or Edexcel, the assessment criteria and conditions for awarding achievement will be very clear. Check each year to make sure that you have kept up to date with any changes. Boards usually have newsletters, websites and training events, which alert practitioners to proposed amendments and the dates of their implementation. Students on award-bearing courses will have assessments and tutorials timetabled into their programmes, and standardized course records to map their learning progress. This has seldom been the case with non-accredited provision.

Non-qualification-bearing courses

The LSC, along with inspectorates,[3] have been concerned to find ways of recognizing and recording progression and achievement in non-accredited learning (RARPA). This has been driven by two needs: first, as robust evidence to claim the achievement element of LSC funding; and second, as a quality assurance measure.

The RARPA approach consists of the application of an explicit and common staged process for the recognition and recording of student learning progress and achievement, together with the validation of this process. It provides evidence for course review. Judgements about its consistent and effective application should be made as part of institutional self-assessment.

The approach supports the delivery of 'Success for All' (DfES 2002).[4] In particular, it is an important part of the comprehensive range of success measures introduced by the DfES throughout the learning and skills sector from September 2005.[5] It also supports the delivery of the Skills Strategy (DfES 2003), which recognized the importance of non-accredited provision in supporting the skills necessary for both employability and social inclusion.

Providers using RARPA are positive about the process, because they have experienced the way it supports quality improvement and promotes good practice and consistency across provision. It allows student achievement to be evidenced for the benefit of learners, which also helps in inspection.

From the student perspective, the RARPA approach is empowering and offers equal esteem for learning acquired through a range of different types of provision in the sector. Providers using the system have reported that students are enthusiastic about setting goals and following progress towards them, and that this has resulted in better motivation and faster progress. It seems to be especially effective at developing confidence and positive attitudes with learners who have previously had negative experiences of education or training. It can also give them a permanent record of their achievement to use as APL towards accreditation or to support a job application. The RARPA standards are to be extended to accredited learning (REX) from 2006/7.

The staged RARPA process[6]

The five elements of the staged process are linked explicitly to key parts of the *Common Inspection Framework*. These five elements are:

1. Aims appropriate to an individual learner or group of learners.
2. Initial assessment to establish the learners' starting points.
3. Identification of appropriately challenging learning objectives: initial, renegotiated and revised.
4. Recognition and recording of progress and achievement during programme (formative assessment): lecturer feedback to learners, learner reflection, progress reviews.
5. End of programme learner self-assessment; tutor summative assessment review of overall progress and achievement. This will be in relation to appropriately challenging learning objectives identified at the beginning of/during the programme. It may include recognition of learning outcomes not specified during the programme.

The lecturer and RARPA/REX

Generally, RARPA follows good practice in teaching and learning and is nothing new. What is new is the application of a total approach to measuring student progression in non-accredited provision. Every organization will have its own way of implementing RARPA, and in order for it to be 'fit for purpose' there are likely to be variations at programme or course level. However, these are some key points for lecturers:

- Ensure your practice is learner-focused, flexible and fit for purpose.
- Present the RARPA approach to learners as an integral part of the process of teaching and learning and not an 'add-on that management want'. This can be a challenge

with older learners, who may think the process of measuring their learning is irrelevant to their needs.

- The staged process can be implemented in all curriculum areas, although some activity-based subjects such as swimming or yoga require creative approaches.
- Evidence of learning does not need to be overly paper-based and certainly students should not be required to write reams.
- Unanticipated outcomes (i.e. things that students gained but that were not part of the course or their own objectives) can be significant, but may not always be appropriate to record formally, e.g. being more tolerant of people from other cultures, or better personal care.
- Use the process to celebrate your students' achievements in college and outside, which encourages new people to return to education. This might include: student/organization newsletter, college website, exhibition with 'portraits and words' about individual or group achievements, an Adult Learners' Week event or award, or a 'human interest story' in the local press.
- Share successful strategies with colleagues.[7]
- Use discussions with your students about their learning to modify your own practice and make the course more relevant and effective.

Identifying students' starting points

Initial assessment
Whether our students are on accredited or non-accredited programmes, we need to find out their starting points so that we can place them on the most appropriate course for their current skills (don't forget, lack of practice can result in deterioration, so don't go by past achievement only). Most FE colleges now do initial testing of all students' basic skills in order to provide appropriate support (see Chapter 4). If you teach a specialist subject, your department may also carry out initial tests, and request a portfolio of work or an audition.

In less formal settings, such as adult community learning or widening participation projects, the idea of subjecting a non-confident or reluctant potential student to a 'test' may appear to be a disastrous strategy. However, the chances are that in the first session you are already making some kind of individual initial assessment. The missing aspect may be that you are not doing it methodically with each person and agreeing their learning needs; or not committing your analysis to a paper record so that you can talk to your students about their progress.

Informal initial assessment

Here are some tried and tested ways of identifying student starting points over the first few classes which can be adapted for your own courses. They are especially useful for direct-entry students and community projects containing students with low literacy.

- In a drawing class set an initial objective drawing task. As you go round to each student, talk to them about their prior experience and their aspirations, judge their current strengths and areas to work on and record this. Ask them to keep this first piece and then compare it with a later drawing, using criteria such as quality of line or composition. You could also photograph it.

- In a humanities class have a discussion in groups about a relevant and preferably controversial topic, e.g. should there be more censorship of the media? As you go round the groups, you can ask students questions about the topic but also about their prior knowledge of the subject and learning goals to form the basis of their individual records.

- Use a short questionnaire on your subject which lists some skills and knowledge related to the course and asks students if they have done this before and if they still feel confident about what they know or can do. This can be done in Makaton[8] for students with learning disabilities or hearing impairment (see box below).

Initial Assessment (Makaton)

Computers Made Easy

I have done this before   I feel confident about this

I can use spell check

I can do basic word processing

I can use spreadsheets

I can scroll up and down

I can open files and use tools

I can save my work

I can use cut and paste

Name of student _____

Feedback about learning

Formative assessment

In order to recognize achievement, assessment must take place and this can seem a very threatening thing for adult students. Research (Greenwood and Wilson 2004) indicates that learners prefer the term 'feedback' to 'assessment' and that their capacity for reflection and self-assessment would be enhanced by more dialogue with lecturers, and the sharing of criteria and norms used to evaluate progress and achievement. It is important that measuring individual achievement does not end up with students competing against each other. This tends to be associated with attainment levels in coursework. Students often see group assessment as threatening to relationships in the class and group cohesion. As discussed earlier, the feeling of 'belonging' and of having peer support can be the difference between a student staying or leaving a course. With some creativity, you may be able to identify group assignments. Indeed, some syllabuses require teamworking to be assessed. It is how assessment and feedback is done that counts.

On qualification courses, there will be a range of practical and written assignments, and perhaps work experience that will need to be assessed and documented according to the accrediting body requirements. Feedback will include: day-to-day informal exchanges; written comments on coursework; and recorded tutorials.

Non-accredited courses have seldom had assessment, and feedback has tended to comprise informal oral comments. RARPA now requires more evidencing of learning progress. Possible evidence includes:

- Group and peer assessment, which could be the written or taped discussion evaluating an exhibition or performance or a video of the 'crit' at the end of an art class – the comments need to be recorded for each individual.
- A record of learner self-assessment which could be written or on a video/audio tape (mobile phones are great for this). Makaton can be used with SLDD students. Photographs need to be annotated, as a visual record alone is not really adequate to evidence the underpinning knowledge required to produce the end product.
- Lecturer record of assessment activities and individual/ group progress and achievement.
- Learners' files, journals, diaries, portfolios, artwork, videos, audiotape, photographs.

- Oral feedback or brief written feedback can be elicited, e.g. start the session by asking each student how they have used x skill or y concept since the last lesson, or use the One-Minute Paper (see box below).

The One-Minute Paper

A world-famous guest conductor was rehearsing with an orchestra of students for a concert at the Barbican Concert Hall. He had no time to learn 80 or more individual names, but wanted to build his relationship with them in order to produce the best possible results. At the end of the first day, he gave each student a piece of paper and asked them to write down the most important thing they had learnt and one thing that would transform the experience for them. He then collected the papers in.

The student who told me this story said that she wrote that rehearsing for hours in a dark college hall when there was bright sunshine outside made her feel depressed. She was amazed to find the next morning that the hall was flooded with light, as the blinds had been pulled back. It changed the group atmosphere and made her feel valued.

This technique is sometimes known as the 'one-minute paper' or 'half-sheet response'.[9] The questions are typically: What is the most important thing that you learnt in class today? And what question is left unanswered? The questions can obviously be changed to fit the situation. The respondents can sign their responses or they can be anonymous. The potential benefits of this technique in relation to RARPA are significant: the sheets are quick to complete and do not cut into teaching time; they encourage students to reflect on their learning; they can be used as evidence of learning progress; they allow unconfident students who might not ask questions in public to give feedback; and they allow us to quickly check that individual students have understood concepts and identify knowledge gaps. Incomplete or incorrect understanding can be addressed with the group at the start of the next

---

lesson, along with recapping key points, or discussed pri-
vately on an individual basis, as appropriate. It may be less
useful with students who have poor language or literacy
skills, although the informality of the process may still
encourage them to have a go. A minimalist version is to ask
the students to write their feedback on Post-It notes. You
will need to judge the appropriateness of this technique
and how often to use it with particular student groups.

Discussing achievement with students

Students need regular, effective feedback in order to make
learning progress and develop confidence and self-esteem.
Wherever possible, they should be involved in self-assessment
using the assessment criteria for the assignment. Careful use of
'question–and–answer' helps them to identify for themselves
what they have learned and areas for development. As discussed
in Chapter 6, adult students' prior experience of education or
training can affect their ability to receive, own and act on
feedback so we need to get it right.[10] The box below has some
hints on giving feedback to adults. Obviously, some aspects are
more appropriate for accredited courses.

Characteristics of effective feedback for adults

- Be clear about what is required in the project briefs and
  include assessment criteria. If appropriate, include the
  characteristics of a piece of work at each grade.
- Establish with students what feedback they can expect.
- Give feedback as soon as possible after the activity.
- If you are giving critical feedback, be prepared that the
  learner may blame you rather than analyse the content
  of the feedback (although praise is usually owned).[11]
- Even if the work is excellent, make suggestions about
  taking it to an even higher level.
- Encourage students to self-assess. They are often more
  critical than you would be. If they have already

evaluated their work against the criteria, your feedback should be easier to take on board. Some subjects such as art and design also use group criticism.

- If a student becomes angry or upset, maintain a professional demeanour and conceal your own emotions. If you can appear cool and focused, this will help the student 'hear' what you have to say.
- Ensure that feedback is balanced, with recognition of good work and ways to improve less good work clearly identified. End with something positive.
- Offer written feedback as well as tutorial discussion so that students who find oral processing difficult can return to your comments and act on them later.
- Focus discussion on the work rather than on the student. In expressive subjects such as visual and performing arts, separating 'the personal' may be more difficult, although there will also be technical points to assess.
- Seek feedback yourself. Do students find your comments useful? How could you improve tutorials or written assessments?
- Explain to students what internal verification processes are used and how to appeal about an assessment. Don't be defensive. The chances are that the more transparent the process is, the less likely students will feel it is unfair.

Summative assessment

Summative assessment is the lecturer's end-of-course assessment of overall progress and achievement by individual students. Systems on award-bearing courses are well known, and include examinations and coursework that result in the student having a certificate indicating a national level of achievement, perhaps a portfolio of work and a reference to support progress to employment or further study.

Evidencing learning progress on non-accredited courses has been less tangible but the development of RARPA will mean that judgements are made in relation to progress against individual learning plans and that there is a record. Evidence on which to make these judgements is the same as detailed under formative assessment, but could also include end-of-course exhibitions and performances. However, again, these would need to identify the knowledge underpinning the event as well as demonstrating improved practical skills and aesthetics. Final assessments might also include unplanned learning outcomes that were significant to the student.

Progression

ALI has identified that progression beyond the current course is often not viewed as an achievement by the lecturer or learner and is therefore given insufficient emphasis or support, for example, post-course advice and guidance. This is perhaps not as true of adults in FE as it is in other parts of the learning and skills sector, but it is worth reflecting on whether we personally do enough, especially with part-time students. Do we rely on the information and guidance team? Are employers or higher education establishments involved in the course and eager to recruit students from it? Could we develop community contacts so that those students who cannot find employment can gain experience as volunteers, thus adding to their CVs and enhancing their chances of getting a good job? After all the hard work that we and our students have put in, we need to ensure that their progress continues.

'Lizzie' left my college with a qualification and a portfolio of work to take her to the next stage, but the most important thing she left with was the confidence to take that next step:

> When I came I had no self-confidence at all. I felt totally wretched. I didn't even like myself. I had lost my job because my husband harassed me at work. That's what drove me to get a divorce in the end. It was awful, I had such low esteem then. The last couple of years I've felt a much stronger person. I think the college has done that for me.

For me, that is what teaching adults is all about.

Notes

[1] Adult educators know this, but, given the emphasis on qualifications, it is interesting to note that it is also recognized in the ALI Chief Inspector's report for 2004 (see website).

[2] Further reading on assessment in FE includes Ecclestone (2002).

[3] ALI reports identify the recognition and recording of achievement as an area of weakness in a range of provision.

[4] *Success for All* (LSC 2002) commits the government to developing a comprehensive set of measures of learner success that can be applied to all provision in the learning and skills sector, including non-accredited learning in colleges, community and workplace. This will be extended by Framework for Excellence (LSC) consultations due August 2006.

[5] A coherent set of success measures aimed at recognizing and celebrating learners' achievements and evaluating the effectiveness of providers across the sector. For adults these include: retention and achievement; learner satisfaction; value added; and distance travelled.

[6] From the evaluation report on the RARPA projects: Greenwood and Wilson 2004.

[7] See www.lsc.gov.uk.rarpa

[8] Makaton is an internationally recognized communication programme based on British Sign Language. It uses symbols to support the written word (see www.makaton.org/).

[9] For further discussion of this technique see Stead (2005: 118).

[10] See *Stress Management in FE* by Elizabeth Hartney in this series for strategies to manage your own feelings and those of your students when giving feedback.

[11] See Smith and King 2004.

Appendix I Abbreviations and acronyms

ACL	Adult Community Learning
ALI	Adult Learning Inspectorate
ALS	Additional Learning Support
AOC	Association of Colleges
BECTA	British Educational Communications and Technology Agency
BPLN	Black Practitioners' and Learners' Network (NIACE)
BSA	Basic Skills Agency
BTEC	Business and Technology Education Council
CBI	Confederation of British Industry
CEL	Centre for Excellence in Leadership
CIF	Common Inspection Framework
CLLP	Central London Learning Partnership
COSHH	Control of Substances Hazardous to Health
COVE	Centre of Vocational Excellence
CRE	Council for Racial Equality
CSW	Communication Support Worker
DDA	Disability Discrimination Act
DfEE	Department for Education and Employment (replaced by DfES)
DFES	Department for Education and Skills
DRC	Disability Rights Commission
DWP	Department of Work and Pensions
E2E	Entry to Employment
EDEXCEL	Incorporates BTEC and London Examinations
EDIM	Equality and Diversity Impact Measure (LSC)
EE	Employer Engagement
EOC	Equal Opportunities Commission
ESF	European Social Fund
ESOL	English for Speakers of Other Languages

EU	European Union
FE	Further Education
FEFC	Further Education Funding Council
FHE	Further and Higher Education
GCE	General Certificate in Education (replaced by GCSE)
GNVQ	General National Vocational Qualification
HE	Higher Education
HESA	Higher Education Statistics Agency
HMI	Her Majesty's Inspectorate
IAG	Information, Advice and Guidance
ILR	Individualized Learner Record
ILT	Information Learning Technology
LEA	Local Education Authority
LLN	Language, Literacy and Numeracy
LLUK	Lifelong Learning UK
LSC	Learning and Skills Council
LSDA	Learning and Skills Development Agency
LSRC	Learning and Skills Research Centre
NALS	National Adult Learner Survey
NAPA	National Association for Providers of Activities for Older People
NBM	Network For Black Managers
NETP	National Employer Training Pilots
NHS	National Health Service
NIACE	National Institute of Adult Continuing Education
NOCN	National Open College Network
NQF	National Qualification Framework
NVQ	National Vocational Qualification
NYA	National Youth Agency
OCN	Open College Network
ODPM	Office for the Deputy Prime Minister
OFSTED	Office for Standards in Education
QCA	Qualifications and Curriculum Authority
QIA	Quality Improvement Agency
RARPA	Recognising and Recording Progression and Achievement
RCU	Responsive College Unit

RDA	Regional Development Agency
REX	RARPA Extension Project
RNIB	Royal National Institute for the Blind
RNID	Royal National Institute for the Deaf
RSA	Royal Society of Art
S4L	Skills for Life (Basic Skills)
SLDD	Students with Learning Difficulties and/or Disabilities
SME	Small and Medium-Sized Enterprises
TEC	Training Enterprise Council
T2G	Train to Gain (National Employer Training Programme)
U3A	University of the Third Age
UCAS	University Central Admissions Service
WBL	Work Based Learning
YALP	Young Adults Learning Partnership

Appendix II Useful organizations and websites

General good practice

Adult Learning Inspectorate's Excalibur website
www.ali.gov.uk/excalibur
Provides case studies with proven methods and techniques from inspection findings in order to raise standards across the learning and skills sector.

Association of Colleges
www.aoc.co.uk/aoc/quality-information/advice
Helpline: 020 7827 4611
Free good practice quality packs (downloadable).

National Institute of Adult Continuing Education
www.niace.org.uk
Produces a monthly magazine, *Adults Learning*, with articles by practitioners, information on current policy developments, publication reviews and information on forthcoming events. Spans FE and ACL. Also publishes *Studies in the Education of Adults*, which contains academic papers relating to adult learning. This is interesting if you are studying for a Cert Ed, but of limited practical use for the busy lecturer. NIACE also publishes some excellent books on adult learning. A really useful website, with links to others.

Quality Improvement Agency
www.qia.org.uk
The QIA has been set up by the government as part of the 'Success for All' programme to speed up quality improvement, increase participation and raise standards and achievement. The website includes updates on progress and details of publications and events.

Equality and diversity

Age Concern
www.ageconcern.org.uk
Information line and fact sheets for older people and professionals.
Includes local services and activities.

Age Positive (Department for Work and Pensions)
www.agepositive.gov.uk
A range of useful information and guidance on age diversity in the
workplace, including news on legislation, good practice guidance and
case studies.

Black Practitioners' and Learners' Network (NIACE)
www.niace.org.uk/BPLN
The network aims to bring together practitioners who are working with
black and minority ethnic group people in order to share good practice
and to discuss and respond to national policies and legislation that impact
on the education of adults. The website has information to support the
further development of skills, knowledge and good practice and to
encourage debate and discussion.

Commission for Racial Equality
www.cre.gov.uk
Information to help tackle racial discrimination and promote race
equality. Education publications focus more on schools than on adult
learning, but good links to other websites with useful resources.

Disability Rights Commission
www.drc-gb.org
The DRC was set up to help secure equal rights for people with disabilities. This service offers practical guidance to employers and organizations such as FE colleges to ensure that people with disabilities are
treated fairly.

Equal Opportunities Commission
www.eoc.org.uk
Gives authoritative advice on a wide range of equality issues, but not
focused on teaching and learning.

Hearing Concern
www.hearingconcern.org.uk
Hearing Concern provides information on communicating with, and equipment for, people who are hard of hearing.

Help the Aged
www.helptheaged.org.uk
In addition to information about local support services, their research publications provide useful information as a teaching resource.

National Autistic Society
www.nas.org.uk
NAS champions the rights and interests of all people with autism and ensures that they and their families receive the quality services that they need. The website provides details about all the training and information services that NAS offers.

Network for Black Managers
www.nbm.org.uk
NBM aims to develop an organization that addresses the needs of black learners, managers and other sector workers, raises awareness of race issues and promotes equality of opportunity within the LSC sectors in England and internationally. Their activities include: professional development activities such as mentoring, coaching, conferences and seminars; lobbying; dissemination of good practice; and research.

Older and Bolder, NIACE
www.niace.org.uk/research/older_bolder
A rich source of information on teaching and learning with older people. Excellent links to other websites.

Partially Sighted Society
Tel: 01302 323 132
http://jim.leeder.users.btopenworld.com/LHON/uk-pss.htm
PSS provides information and advice on making the environment more accessible to people who are partially sighted.

Race Equality and Diversity Unit, Home Office
http://communities.homeoffice.gov.uk/raceandfaith
The Race, Cohesion, Equality and Faith Directorate works with other government departments to reduce race and faith inequalities in educa-tion, health, housing and the Criminal Justice System, as well as the

labour market. Helpful at policy level and with grants for social cohesion projects rather than classroom materials.

Royal National Institute for the Blind
www.rnib.org.uk
Text: 0800 515 152
RNIB offers information, support and advice to people with sight problems. RNIB also works with organizations to enable them to improve the accessibility of websites, information, products, services and the built environment for people with sight problems.

Royal National Institute for Deaf People
www.rnid.org.uk
RNID provides information and resources for deaf and hard of hearing people, their families, friends, employers and professionals. There is information about deafness and hearing loss, the latest products and equipment such as hearing aids, induction loops and text phones, and useful tips to help you communicate better with people with hearing difficulties.

Skill: National Bureau for Students with Disabilities
www.skill.org.uk
Tel: 020 7450 0620 (voice/text)
Skill is a charity that promotes opportunities for young people and adults with any kind of disability in post-16 education, training and employment across the UK.

Social Exclusion Unit, Office of the Deputy Prime Minister
www.socialexclusionunit.gov.uk
SEU works closely with other parts of the ODPM, such as the Neighbourhood Renewal Unit and the Homelessness and Housing Support Directorate, to tackle deprivation. Useful facts and figures, research and policy papers on working with disadvantaged adults.

Young Adults Learning Partnership (YALP)
www.niace.org.uk/research/YALP
A joint initiative between NIACE and the National Youth Agency. The partnership researches and develops effective approaches to learning and personal development among young adults aged 16 to 25 who are on the margins of education, training and employment.

Good practice in relation to employers

Business in the Community
www.bitc.org.uk/resources
This organization works with companies to improve the positive impact of business in society.

Department for Trade and Industry
www.dti.gov.uk/bestpractice
This website offers an interesting variety of best practice on a wide range of business issues.

Appendix III Bibliography

Afshar, H. (1994) 'Muslim women in West Yorkshire: growing up with real and imaginary values amidst conflicting views of self and society' in H. Afshar and M. Maynard (eds) *The Dynamics of 'Race' and Gender: Some Feminist Interventions*. London: Taylor and Francis.

Aldridge, F. and Tuckett, A. (2004) *Business as Usual? NIACE Survey of Adult Participation*. Leicester: NIACE.

Aldridge, F. and Tuckett, A. (2005) *Better News this Time: NIACE Survey of Adult Participation*. Leicester: NIACE.

Allan, G. (1989) *Friendships: Developing a Sociological Perspective*. Brighton: Harvester/Wheatsheaf.

Allan, G. (1990) 'Insiders and outsiders: boundaries around the home' in G. Allan and G. Crow (eds) *Home and Family: Creating the Domestic Sphere*. Basingstoke: Macmillan.

Association of Colleges (2006) Powering the Nation's Skills briefing paper for Westminster Hall debate, 2 Feb 2006. London: AOC.

Audit Commission/Ofsted (1993) *Unfinished Business: Full-time Educational Courses for 16–19-year-olds*. London: HMSO.

Bargh, C., Scott, P. and Smith, D. (1994) *Access and Consolidation: The Impact of Reduced Student Intakes on Opportunities for Non-standard Applicants*. Leeds: Centre for Policy Studies in Education, University of Leeds.

Benn, R. (1998) 'Still struggling' in R. Benn, J. Elliot and P. Whalley *Educating Rita and her Sisters: Women and Continuing Education*. Leicester: NIACE.

Bhavnani, K.K. (1993) 'Tracing the contours: feminist research and feminist objectivity', *Women's Studies International Forum*, 16 (2): 95–104.

Bourdieu, P. (1977) *Outline of a Theory of Practice*. Cambridge: Cambridge University Press.

Bourdieu, P. (1982) *Lecon sur la lecon*. Paris: Editions de Minuit.

Bourdieu, P. and Passeron, J.-C. (1990) *Reproduction, Education, Society and Culture*. London: Sage.

Bourdieu, P. and Wacquant, L. (1992) *An Invitation to Reflexive Sociology*. London: Polity Press.

Centre for Excellence in Leadership (2005) *Leading Change in Equality and Diversity*. London: CEL.

Champney, J., Davey, M. and Lawrence, S. (2005) *Breaking Down the Barriers: Success in Widening Participation, a Toolkit Approach*. London: LSDA.

Coffield, F., Moseley, D., Hall, E. and Ecclestone, K. (2004) *Learning Styles for Post-16 Learners: What do We Know? A Review of Literature on Learning Styles and Pedagogy in Post-Sixteen Learning*. London: LSRC.

Colley, H., James, D., Tedder, M. and Diment, K. (2003) 'Learning as becoming in vocational education and training: class, gender and the role of vocational habitus', *Journal of Vocational Education and Training*, 55 (4): 471–97.

Cullen, M. A. (1994) *Weighing It Up: A Case Study of Discontinuing Access Students*. Edinburgh: University of Edinburgh, Centre for Continuing Education.

Deere, J., Gardener, S. and Jude, C. (1997) 'Time well spent', *Adults Learning* 8 (9): 249–51.

Dench, S. and Regan, J. (2000) 'Learning in later life: motivation and impact', Research report 183. London: DfEE.

Department for Education and Employment (DfEE) (1995) *Lifetime Learning: A Consultation Document*. London: HMSO.

Department for Education and Employment (DfEE) (1998) *The Learning Age*, London: HMSO.

Department of Education and Science (DfES) (1991) *Student Completion Rates in Further Education*. HMI Report 281/91. London: DES.

Department for Education and Skills (DfES) (2002) *Success for All: Reforming Further Education and Training*. London, DfES.

Department for Education and Skills (DfES) (2003) *21st Century Skills: Realising our Potential*. London: HMSO.

Ecclestone, K. (2002) *Learning Autonomy in Post-16 Education: The Politics and Practice of Formative Assessment*. London: Routledge Falmer.

Edwards, R. (1993) *Mature Women Students: Separating or Connecting Family and Education*. Portsmouth: Taylor and Francis.

Feinstein, L., Hammond, C., Woods, L., Preston, J. and Bynner, J. (2003) *The Contribution of Adult Learning to Health and Social Capital*. London: Institute of Education.

Fieldhouse, R. (1998) *A History of Modern British Adult Education*. Leicester: NIACE.

Finch, J. (1983) 'Dividing the rough and the respectable: working-class women and pre-school playgroups' in E. Gamarnikow, D. Morgan, J.

Purvis and D. Taylorson (eds) *The Public and the Private*. London: Heinemann.

Foster, A. (2005) *Realising the Potential: A Review of the Future Role of Further Education Colleges*. Nottingham: DfES.

Foucault, M. (1977) *The Archaeology of Knowledge*. London: Tavistock.

Frank, F. and Houghton, G. (1997) 'When life gets in the way', *Adults Learning* 8 (9): 244–5.

Further Education Funding Council (FEFC) (The Widening Participation Committee) (1997) *Pathways to Success: Emerging Conclusions* (known as the Kennedy Report). Coventry: FEFC.

Further Education Funding Council (FEFC) (1998) *The Inclusive Learning Quality Initiative Stage 2*. Circular 98/31. Coventry: FEFC.

Gerwitz, S., Ball, S. and Bowe, R. (1995) *Markets, Choice and Equity in Education*. Buckingham: Open University Press.

Greenwood, M., Merton, A. and Taylor, S. (2000) *An Evaluation of Non-Schedule 2 Pilot Projects*. London: LSDA.

Greenwood, M. and Wilson, P. (2004) *Recognising and Recording Progress and Achievement in Non-Accredited Learning*. Leicester: NIACE.

Hayes, A. (1999) *Making the Future: Women Students in the New Further Education*. London: Kings College, London (PhD thesis).

Hillier, Y. and Jameson, J. (2003) *Researching Post-compulsory Education*. London: Continuum.

Hodkinson, P. and James, D. (2003) 'Transforming learning cultures in further education', *Journal of Vocational Education and Training* 55 (4): 389–406.

Hodkinson, P. (2005) *Improving Learning in Further Education: a new cultural approach*. TLRB no. 12; www.tlrp.org/pub/documents/Hodkinson RBFinal.pdf

Hughes, C. (chair) (2005) *Eight in Ten Learners in Further Education*. Report of the independent committee of enquiry set up by NIACE. Leicester: NIACE.

James, D. and Diment, K. (2003) 'Learning and assessment in an ambiguous space', *Journal of Vocational Education and Training* 55 (4): 407–22.

Janssen, R. (2004) 'Learning while caring', *Adults Learning* 16 (2): 12–13. Leicester: NIACE.

Kelly, T. (1992) *A History of Adult Education in Great Britain*. Liverpool: Liverpool University Press.

Kember, D. (1995) *Open Learning Courses for Adults: A Model of Student Progress*. Englewood Cliffs, New Jersey: Education Technology Publications.

Lave, J. and Wenger, E. (1991) *Situated Learning*. Cambridge: Cambridge University Press.

Learning and Skills Council (LSC) (2002) *National Equality and Diversity Strategy 2001–2004*. Coventry: LSC.

Learning and Skills Council (2002) *Success for all*. Coventry: LSC.

Learning and Skills Council (LSC) (2003) *Successful Participation for All: Widening Adult Participation Strategy*. Coventry: LSC.

Learning and Skills Council (2004) *Measuring Success in the Learning Skills Sector*. Coventry: LSC.

Lloyd, B. and Duveen, G. (1992) *Gender Identities and Education*. London: Harvester Wheatsheaf.

Luttrell, W. (1993) 'The teachers, they all had their pets: concepts of gender, knowledge and power', *Signs: Journal of Women's Culture and Society*, 18 (3): 505–46.

McGivney, V. (1990) *Education's for Other People: Access to Education for Non-participant Adults*. Leicester: NIACE.

McGivney, V. (1996) *Staying or Leaving the Course*. Leicester: NIACE.

McPherson, W. (1999) *The Stephen Lawrence Inquiry: Report of an Inquiry by Sir William McPherson of Cluny*. London: Stationery Office.

Mansell, P. and Parkin, C. (1990) 'Student Drop Out: A Handbook for Managers'. Unpublished report from FEU project RP539: Student Participation and Wastage: from Research to Practice.

Martinez, P. (1995) 'Student retention in further and adult education: the evidence,' Mendip Papers 084. London: FEDA.

Martinez, P. (1997) *Improving Student Retention: A Guide to Successful Strategies*. London: FEDA.

Maynard, M. (1994) 'Race, gender and the concept of difference in feminist thought' in H. Afshar and M. Maynard (eds) *The Dynamics of 'Race' and Gender: Some Feminist Interventions*. London: Taylor and Francis.

Moore, R. (1995) *Retention Rates Research Project: Final Report*. Sheffield: Division of Access and Guidance, Sheffield Hallam University.

Morrison, M. (1992) 'Part-time: whose time? Women's lives and adult learning' in R. Edwards, A. Hanson and P. Raggatt (1996) *Boundaries of Adult Learning*. London: Routledge/OU.

Munn, P., MacDonald, C. and Lowden, K. (1992) *Helping Adult Students Cope*. Scottish Council for Research in Education.

O'Rourke, R. (1995) 'All equal now?' in M. Mayo and J. Thompson (eds) *Adult Learning Critical Intelligence and Social Change*. Leicester: NIACE.

Owens, J. and Davies, P. (2003) *Listening to Staff 2002*. London: LSDA.

Payne, J. and Edwards, R. (1997) 'Impartiality in pre-entry guidance for adults in further education colleges', *British Journal of Guidance and Counselling* 25 (3): 361–75.

Phoenix, A. (1987) 'Theories of gender and black families', in G. Weiner and M. Arnot (eds) *Gender Under Scrutiny: New Inquiries in Education.* London: Hutchinson.

Qualifications and Curriculum Authority (QCA) (2004) *A Framework for Achievement: Recognising Qualifications and Skills in the 21st Century.* London: QCA.

Reay, D. (1996) 'Dealing with difficult differences: reflexivity and social class in feminist research', *Feminism and Psychology*, 6 (3): 443–56.

Reay, D. (1998) ' "Always Knowing" and "never being sure": familial and institutional habituses and higher education choice', *Journal of Education Policy*, 13 (4): 519–29.

Reisenberger, A. and Sadler, J. (1997) *On Course for Next Steps: Careers Education and Guidance in Colleges.* London: FEDA.

Robertson, H. J. (1992) 'Teacher development and gender equity' in A. Hargreaves and M. G. Fullan (eds) *Understanding Teacher Development.* New York: Teachers College Press, Columbia University, Cassell.

Scottish Education Department/HMI (1992) *Measuring Up: Performance Indicators in Further Education.* SOED.

Smith, C. and King, P. (2004) 'Student feedback sensitivity and the efficacy of feedback interventions in public speaking performance improvement', *Communication Education*, 53 (3): 3–216.

Smith, G. and Bailey, V. (1993) *Staying the Course.* London: BTEC.

Social Exclusion Unit (2004) *Mental Health and Social Exclusion.* West Yorkshire: ODPM Publications.

Stasz, C. and Wright, S. (2004) *Emerging Policy for Vocational Learning in England. Will it Lead to a Better System?* London: Learning and Skills Research Centre.

Stead, D. (2005) 'A review of the one-minute paper', *Active Learning in Higher Education*, 6 (2): 118–31.

Tait, T. (2003) *Credit Systems for Learning and Skills: Current Developments.* London: LSDA.

Taylor, S., Macleod, D., Houghton, N. and Zwart, R. (2004) *A Systematic Review of Effective Strategies to Widen Adult Participation in learning.* Draft online report on EPPI. London: Institute of Education, University of London.

Walhberg, M. and Gleeson, D. (2003) 'Doing the business: paradox and irony in vocational education – GNVQ Business Studies as a case in point', *Journal of Vocational Education and Training*, 55 (4): 42–5.

Weiner, G. and Maguire, M. (1995) 'No age is the right age for a woman' in E. Befring (ed.) *Teacher Education for Equality*. Conference Proceedings of the Association for Teacher Education in Europe. Norway: Oslo College.

Wertsch, J. V. (1998) *Mind and Action*. New York: Oxford University Press.

Withnall, A., McGivney, V. and Soulsby, J. (2004) *Older People Learning: Myths and Realities*. Leicester, NIACE.

Index